YO
ELIZABE

CONSTANCE SAVERY

LUTTERWORTH PRESS
GUILDFORD AND LONDON

First published 1954

This paperback edition first published 1975

ISBN 0 7188 2193 9

PRINTED OFFSET LITHO AND BOUND IN GREAT BRITAIN
BY COX & WYMAN LTD
LONDON, FAKENHAM AND READING

CONTENTS

Chapter I

SCHOOL MOTHER ELIZABETH

"FIFTEEN, Elizabeth Green!" called the monitress for the week, standing in the dark arched doorway above the courtyard where the fifty members of Crowgarth's Female Orphanage were taking their afternoon recreation.

"I am coming, Five, Sophia Clive!" answered Fifteen, Elizabeth Green. She tossed the ball to her partner, Ten, Louisa Glenn, and ran across the flags and up the three steps to the great door. As she ran, she wondered which of her faults had found her out. Had her buttonholes failed to satisfy the needlework mistress? Had M. Duclos complained about the concord mistake in her French exercise? Had she forgotten to put some vital ingredient in the Plain Pudding for Poor People that had been the subject of the morning's cookery class?

"What is it, Five, Sophia Clive?" she asked, in a disturbed whisper.

"Nothing, to the best of my knowledge," the monitress answered, unemotionally. "Miss Tadcaster has sent for you, that's all I know. Tidy your hair with your fingers, Fifteen. It's very wild."

Relieved in mind, Elizabeth Green smoothed her curly brown locks carefully before setting out for the private room where Miss Tadcaster interviewed good orphans, bad orphans, their relatives, and their future employers. Long ago, Elizabeth had decided that when she too became the Superintendent of a Female Orphanage, she would have a private room that should be an exact copy of Miss Tadcaster's, from the canary in his cage to the portrait of the white-wigged Founder in his lace ruffles and cherry-coloured coat.

She knocked, and Miss Tadcaster called out, "Enter!" Hanging in his gilt frame on the wall, Mr. Charles Crowgarth gazed as benignly at Elizabeth as he had done on the day when she saw him first.

Miss Tadcaster laid down the letter she had been reading.

"Be seated, Elizabeth," she said gravely.

Elizabeth's heart thumped fast, but not with fear. One stood to be rebuked or admonished. Since a chair had been offered, this could be neither rebuke nor admonition.

She sat down and folded her hands demurely.

"You are aware, Elizabeth," said Miss Tadcaster, "that the funds of this institution do not permit of our retaining all the senior girls to the age of eighteen, to be trained as finishing governesses?"

"Yes, Ma'am."

"Only the six at the head of the second class can hope to remain at Crowgarth's after their sixteenth birthday?"

"Yes, Ma'am."

"What has been your place in the second class, Elizabeth, ever since you joined it, nearly two years ago?"

"I have never risen higher than seventh, Ma'am. I never shall."

"No, Elizabeth, frankly I fear that you never will. Pray understand that your instructresses do not blame you for what cannot properly be termed a failure. You have always been a diligent and persevering pupil, my child, and I have pleasure in telling you that in all your studies you are distinctly in advance of your age. But it has been your lot to contend with six rivals of quite extraordinary gifts. In a long and varied teaching experience, I have never met six more talented young persons. Regretfully, I repeat that you must abandon all hope of excelling any one of them. And so——"

Elizabeth thought that Mr. Charles Crowgarth's friendly gaze was troubled, and she smiled at him to show that he was not to be blamed for the post-war fall in the value of money, any more than she was to be blamed for not being a talented young person of quite extraordinary gifts. When he founded the Orphanage, he hadn't known that England would have to fight Napoleon Bonaparte a hundred years after he was dead.

"—I have decided to accept the offer of a post for you," Miss Tadcaster continued. "True, you are only fifteen—but you have already learnt all that Crowgarth's can teach those who are not going to enter the first class. In the circumstances, I do not wish you to miss the chance of a particularly good post in the family of a lady well known to me by repute, in whose house you will be watched over with motherly care and will be given ample time for the private studies that will qualify you to seek a higher post when you are of an age for such advancement. My widowed acquaintance, Mrs. Deveril of Deveril Court near Falfont St. Philip, requires a governess for a young distant cousin, Miss Donata Deveril, who is, like you, an orphan. Miss Deveril lived first with her grandmother, then with other relatives. She arrived unexpectedly at the Court a few weeks ago. You will teach Scripture, English history, literature and grammar, elementary plain sewing, and the use of the globes. You will also supervise Miss Deveril's pianoforte practice and be present at the lessons she receives from her visiting French, music, arithmetic and deportment masters . . ."

Miss Tadcaster went on talking, and Elizabeth went on listening. At last Elizabeth understood that she was permitted to ask questions. She asked two.

"Has Mrs. Deveril any children of her own, Ma'am?"

Mrs. Deveril has a married daughter and three sons. The eldest manages his estates, the second is an Oxford undergraduate, the third is a schoolboy. I do not know whether any of the sons are at home at present; but if they are, you will see nothing of them. The schoolroom is your province, and you will be expected to remain in it."

"Please, Ma'am, how old is Miss Donata Deveril?"

"I cannot tell you. Mrs. Deveril's letter was written in haste and agitation immediately after hearing that a beloved sister had fallen seriously ill. But I gather that Miss Deveril is quite young, six or seven probably. Her cousin admits with reluctance that she is not only disgracefully ignorant but also 'exceedingly naughty and self-willed'."

"Oh!" said Elizabeth.

"You need not be afraid," said Miss Tadcaster. "Perhaps no one has told you that you have a rare gift in dealing with naughty little children. That is why you have already been appointed—though so young—'school mother' to so many of the babies. Indeed, I do not think we could have kept little Tibbie Marsh among us, had you not helped her to overcome the sad passions implanted during her neglected infancy. Your patience and perseverance have done much towards making her a well-conducted, agreeable little girl."

This was indeed high praise. Hearing it, Elizabeth turned pink.

"I do not anticipate that you will have any difficulty in controlling Donata Deveril," said Miss Tadcaster. "But if you fail—for that or for any other reason—to keep your post at Deveril Court, you will return to Crowgarth until you are sixteen, when we will again endeavour to secure a post for you."

Elizabeth held her curly head high. Never would she endure to be sent back to the Orphanage a failure, like poor Laura Knowles, whom she had so deeply pitied! Never!

"That is all, Elizabeth."

When Elizabeth Green found herself at a safe distance from the other side of the door, she sprang into the air, just to make sure that she was not dreaming. She said to herself in a clear voice:

"I am no longer Fifteen, Elizabeth Green. I shall never be Fifteen—except for my age!—again."

Each of the orphans had a school number, given to her on her arrival and retained by her throughout her stay. *Fifteen* was sewn on every one of Elizabeth's clothes, and *fifteen* was stamped in all her school books. She had come to the Orphanage when she was so small that she had innocently answered "Fifteen" in church when the Vicar asked her the first question in the *Catechism*: What is your name? Later, she had been proud to find that she, like Seven, Mary Bevan, Six, Jane Rix, Sophia, and Louisa, was one of the girls whose number rhymed with their name. Now that glory was childish, to be put aside and forgotten. She was a young woman, going to her first post.

While evening preparation was in progress for their elders, Elizabeth's "babies" stole in from their play to watch their school mother pack part of her tiny store of possessions, and set aside the rest as keepsakes to be given to her friends. She reserved as an appropriate gift for her new pupil the set of coloured paper dolls she had been making for little Tibbie Marsh, and to Tibbie she gave in exchange, not without an inward struggle, the precious necklace of tiny iridescent blue shells that she had treasured all her life. The delight in Tibbie's face almost made up for the sacrifice.

"Oh! Oh! I do believe you've given me the very bestest thing you have!"

The other babies eyed the necklace wistfully, but not covetously. They quite understood that it ought to go to Tibbie, who might have to wait for an unknown length of time before Elizabeth was at leisure to make another set of dolls.

"I shall be a good, good girl for ever because I've got this!" boasted Tibbie, strutting up and down in her necklace. "I shall never bite anybody again."

"You can't be good unless you ask the Lord Jesus to help you," Elizabeth reminded her charges. "That's what my school mother taught me, when I was much smaller than any of you."

"Tell us how your school mother taught you," said Tibbie.

They all knew the story, but they wanted to hear it again. Elizabeth sat down on a long, low blanket-chest and put her arms round as many as she could reach.

"My school mother was Esther Parracombe. She had golden hair and brown eyes, and long, long ago she went away to be a governess. She's married now, and she has a little girl and a little boy. I liked her very, very, very, much. She was the best school mother in the whole world."

"No, she wasn't," said the babies. "She couldn't have been. You are."

Elizabeth laughed, with a shy thrill of pleasure. She cuddled the babies tight, and said:

"Wait till you get your next school mother. I think I know whom Miss Tadcaster will choose out of the second class. She's far, far better than I am. No, no, we won't stop to argue about it. Now, listen! This is my last night, so I want us to say together the first verse my school mother ever taught me. You have learnt it too.

"Loving Jesu, gentle Lamb,
In Thy gracious hands I am.
Make me, Saviour, what Thou art,
Live Thyself within my heart."

"How did we get into His gracious hands?"

inquired Tibbie. "What does it mean? I am not in anybody's hands. Not even in yours, because Betsy pushed into my place. I am sitting on the blanket-chest, and a moth has just gone through that crack in the wood. I saw it."

Elizabeth thought for a moment. "It means that we are all in His loving care for Him to make us good. Once I heard of a little boy of six who made up this beautiful prayer for himself: *Lord Jesus, make me like You when You were six years old.* We—you and I—could pray that prayer, couldn't we?"

"No," said Tibbie. "I'm five. Lucy's four. You are fifteen. Only Betsy and Susan can say it."

"It's a prayer that fits everybody young," said Elizabeth. "You and I and Lucy can turn the little boy's 'six' into five, four and fifteen. Do you think that you could remember to say it every morning and evening?"

"'Lord Jesus, make me like You when You were five years old,'" said Tibbie. "I'll beremember, I promise. And I'll teach Lucy. What was Jesus like when He was five years old? And fifteen?"

Elizabeth hesitated. She knew that they were about to hear the little ones' silence bell, after which all talking was strictly forbidden in the babies' rooms. How could she, in the small remaining time, answer such a question?

"There's a hymn we elder ones sing at evening

prayers," she said. "It will tell you, better than I can. I know the words—I'll sing it. No, I'm afraid you wouldn't understand—it might muddle you."

"'Twouldn't. Nothing couldn't muddle me," said Tibbie.

The first notes of the silence bell began to sound. Elizabeth bent down to kiss her "babies" good night for the last time. "I can't tell you," she whispered, "but *Jesus can.* He will, if you ask Him."

Chapter 2

INTO THE WIDE, WIDE WORLD

BLACK-CLOAKED in readiness for her journey, Elizabeth attended morning prayers before setting off to join the Royal Lion in the market square. To her surprise, they sang the hymn that was usually reserved for evening prayers after the little ones had gone to bed.

"Plant, and root, and fix in me
All the mind that was in Thee;
Settled peace I then shall find;
Jesu's is a *quiet* mind.

Anger I no more shall feel,
Always even, always still,
Meekly on my God reclined;
Jesu's is a *gentle* mind . . ."

sang the Orphanage.

Elizabeth thought that it was a very suitable hymn for a person of fifteen who was stepping from the shelter of school into the unknown world beyond. Miss Tadcaster evidently thought so too; for when at the end of prayers Elizabeth went up to receive the "leaving gifts" of a guinea and a new hymn book, the Superintendent pointed to the lines that had just been sung, saying, gravely and impressively:

"You will find your special 'leaving text' in the second chapter of St. Paul's *Epistle to the Philippians*, verse five: 'Let this mind be in you, which was also in Christ Jesus.'"

Waiting alone for Matron to escort her to the coach, Elizabeth opened her hymn book and read through the nine verses that told how the mind of Christ was quiet, gentle, patient, fearlessly noble, spotless, loving, thankful, constant, perfect.

"And I must be like that when I am teaching Donata," she thought. "A little, little like it, at least. I can't be, any more than the babies could, without His help. I waver and wander, just as the hymn-writer said he did. Oh, please, Lord Jesus—

'Plant, and root, and fix in me
ALL THE MIND that was in Thee.'

Ten minutes later, she was in the coach for Falfont St. Philip, feeling very much like a young thrush that she had once seen pushed out of the nest by the unfeeling parent who was teaching it to fly.

Wedged between two stout fellow-passengers in check shawls, she could see nothing of the countryside through which they were passing. After two hot, stuffy hours had gone by, she was almost too sleepy to go on making plans for work and play with a pupil who would, she felt sure, be just such another dear little girl as her darling lost "babies". Drowsily she pictured herself and a white-clad, blue-ribboned Donata sitting together on a tree-shaded bank above a river. From matches, pins, and acorns she was making a herd of toy piglets driven by a tiny swineherd in a Turkey oak's hairy cap . . . she was fashioning rush rafts for Donata out of reed-maces . . . she was reading aloud to Donata from one of her own early prize-books that she had brought with her in the brown string bag that had been Matron's last gift, from *Jemima Placid*, perhaps, or *Elements of Morality*, or *A Puzzle for a Curious Girl*. . .

Bang! Crash! The string bag slipped from Elizabeth's hand and went flopping and bounding she knew not where. Her nose was buried deep in the black-and-white of a neighbour's shawl, and the rest of her seemed to be entombed beneath two or three mountains. Somewhere above the mountains she heard shouts, screams, angry roars. The world swung and swayed. Then the rocking stopped and the mountains heaved themselves up. Elizabeth, battered and breathless, understood that the occupants of the coach had been flung higgledy-piggledy across one another when the coachman pulled up sharply in a desperate but successful effort to avoid an accident.

"What was it?—what happened?" gasped

Elizabeth, shielding her bruised face with her hand.

Angry voices answered that two madcap riders had leapt a hedge into the highway almost under the horses' heads. Dashing across the road without paying the smallest attention to their own danger or their victims' distress, they had galloped half way across the next county by now.

"But I know who one of them was!" roared an angry farmer, turning round from the window to shake his fist at his fellow sufferers instead of at the escaped criminals. "I'll have the law on him for endangering all our lives in a public conveyance. I couldn't see who he'd got with him, but no matter for that! One's enough. And you'll all be able to bear witness that it was Mrs. Deveril's youngest boy!"

"I—I didn't see him," said Elizabeth quickly.

She was very thankful that she could say so. It would have been exceedingly awkward, she reflected, to begin her governess-ship by giving evidence before the magistrates against her employer's third son.

The other passengers regarded her stonily. Their displeasure was even more plainly visible when the coach halted at the entrance to Deveril Court. While her box was being lifted down, she saw them whispering, with cross looks, as though they had guessed why she was unwilling to add her testimony to theirs.

Coming out of his lodge behind the lofty iron

gates, the lodgekeeper listened grinning to all that the coachman, the guard and the passengers had to say. Elizabeth stood meekly by, holding a handkerchief to her cheek. When the coach had rattled off, she made her way up the long drive, the lodgekeeper accompanying her with the box wheeled before him on a barrow.

To Elizabeth's relief, her guide did not take her to the pillared and porticoed front door of stately Deveril Court, but to a side door leading into what he told her was "the schoolroom wing". As they reached the door, it was flung open from within. A worried lady in black rushed out to stand peering distractedly in search of some object that she could not see.

"Mrs. Hunt, the housekeeper, Miss," said the lodgekeeper softly to Elizabeth, who could hardly believe him. Mrs. Hunt's gold chain, black silk gown, and lace cap were more magnificent than Miss Tadcaster's best clothes. Surely the man must have made a mistake! If not a duchess, this could only be Mrs. Deveril herself.

But Mrs. Hunt proclaimed her own identity as she came forward to greet the new-comer in a kindly but flurried manner. "You are the young lady sent by Miss Tadcaster? I am rejoiced to see you. Your pupil, unfortunately, does not appear to be in the house or grounds. I am just going in search of her—naughty Donata! My name is Hunt, Mrs. Hunt. In the absence of Mrs. Deveril, I am in temporary charge of the domestic arrangements of the Court. I shall always be ready to give you any advice or assistance you may require."

"Mrs. Deveril is from home?" said Elizabeth, startled.

"I deeply regret to say that she was summoned yesterday to her sister's bedside. She was disappointed not to be able to receive you; but she is sure that she need have no hesitation in entrusting Donata to the care of any lady sent by Miss Tadcaster, on whose judgment she is fully content to rely. But I am forgetting my duties!—my mind so constantly recurs to the question, what can have become of Donata? Pray come in, Miss——?"

"I am . . . Elizabeth Green," said Elizabeth, just contriving to swallow down "fifteen". "Oh, please, Madam, had I not better go at once in search of Donata?"

"No, it is wiser not. You would have no notion where to seek her. I will attend to the matter myself while you are resting and taking some refreshment after your journey. But, my dear Miss Green, what is the matter? You have hurt your face."

"It is nothing. A trifling accident in the coach," said Elizabeth. "If I could bathe it with cold water——"

"Certainly, certainly. Bring the box, Standing. This way, if you please."

Left alone in a pleasant bedroom with hangings

of white and pink dimity, Elizabeth laved her discoloured face, brushed her hair and unpacked her possessions. Then she made her way to the schoolroom, where the promised tray of refreshments awaited her.

From the windows Elizabeth looked out on the elms, oaks and beeches of the park, all dappled in sunshine. She sat eating her cold chicken, grapes, and cake with pride in her sudden advancement, a pride that began to be mingled with fear. Little runaway Donata promised to be a harder problem to tackle than dear funny Tibbie Marsh!

The meal over, Elizabeth examined her new home, which had been the schoolroom of the one-time Miss Deveril, whose name was written in the Pinnock's *Catechisms*, Mrs. Marcet's *Conversations on Chemistry*, Mangnall's *Questions*, and Lindley Murray's *Grammar* that adorned the long shelves. Traces of the reigning Miss Deveril there were none. If Donata possessed toys and picture-books, she did not keep them here.

Elizabeth bestowed her own books and the packet of paper dolls in an empty bureau that was clearly intended for the governess's use. This done, she stood by the window, hoping for a glimpse of the returning truant's snowy draperies and fluttering blue ribbons, but seeing no one save an aged weeding-woman at work with her basket on the terrace below.

Suddenly, without other warning than the sound of a door banging somewhere on the far side of the wing, a girl of her own age, dressed in a riding-habit, bounded into the room. At sight of Elizabeth, she stopped short.

"Who in the world are you?"

Elizabeth sought to behave with preceptorial dignity.

"May I ask first, who you are?"

"Me? I'm Donnet Deveril."

Elizabeth hid her dismay as well as she could.

"I am your governess, Elizabeth Green."

"That you are not!" said Miss Donata Deveril. "There is a mistake somewhere. My cousin, Mrs. Deveril, wrote to a certain Miss Tadpole, who keeps, I understand, some kind of agency for procuring governesses, and desired her to send the stiffest, starchiest, middle-agedest governess on her list."

"Miss Tadcaster told me that Mrs. Deveril's letter was written in haste and agitation," said poor Elizabeth. "I am sure Mrs. Deveril did not desire a governess to be selected from among the past pupils. She must have forgotten to state her wishes. So—so Miss Tadcaster chose me."

"And where did Miss Tadcaster light on a small creature like you, pray?" said Donata.

"Miss Tadcaster is the Superintendent of Crowgarth Female Orphanage," Elizabeth answered.

"And you are a female orphan?"

"Yes."

"It's intolerable!" said Donata, giving a little leap into the air. "I didn't want an old tabby over me, but I was prepared to put up with her. After all, I've met and worsted dozens of them. But nobody in their senses could expect me to submit to being ruled by an orphan miss no older than myself. An orphan with a black eye, too! I dare say you got it when you were fighting the other misses."

"No, I did not!" cried Elizabeth angrily. "If you must know, I got it when a Master Deveril and his friend dashed on horseback across the road in front of the Royal Lion. There was very nearly an accident. All the passengers were flung topsy-turvy."

"Oh!" said Donata, as if checked. "And how did you know that the rider was Nel—I mean, was one of the Deverils?"

Elizabeth explained.

Donata Deveril stood frowning, pouting, tapping her fingers on the table.

"Tiresome!" she said. "Very tiresome! What an old curmudgeon Farmer Watson is!—and how very unfortunate that he should have been in the coach on the worst possible day! But it doesn't make any difference to what I said before. I refuse to have a mere child put in authority over me. I shall ask my cousin Cosmo —he is my cousin, Mrs. Deveril's, eldest son—to send you back to the Orphanage with a letter explaining the unfortunate mistake."

Elizabeth was pale with wrath. "I have nothing to do with Mr. Cosmo Deveril. I was engaged by his mother, Mrs. Deveril, and I take my orders from her."

"Absurd!" said Donata. "This is Cosmo's house, and Cosmo isn't a boy, he's twenty-one. Everybody obeys Cosmo—and you will too! I shall speak to him at once, before that wretch Farmer Watson comes lumbering round to lodge complaints. Oh, Nel, you're lurking in the passage, are you? Didn't know you were there. How much have you heard?"

"Everything," said Nel, advancing into the room.

"This is Mrs. Deveril's son, Nelmont," said Donata stiffly. "Miss Green."

Elizabeth curtsied. She could not doubt that the boy of sixteen was the youngest son, and she began to entertain an uncomfortable suspicion that his companion in the cross-country ride had been none other than Miss Donata Deveril.

"Then I am quite sure you agree with me that it's out of the question that Miss Green should stay here as my governess," said Donata, with a pettish stamp of her foot. "Taught by a girl of my own age!—it's ludicrous! I should be the laughing-stock of the neighbourhood."

"One moment," said Nelmont. "Give me time to apologize to Miss Green for the unintentional damage I did this morning. Indeed, I am very sorry, Miss Green. As for you, Donnet," he added, turning to his cousin, "you are a bufflehead with no manners at all. I am sure that Miss Green knows ten times as much as you do, and that—always providing she can bring herself to stay here after your rude treatment—she will teach you a great deal. You had better ask pardon for your crimes as gracefully as you can."

"I won't!"

"You're not only an unmannerly bufflehead you're a short-sighted bufflehead. Remarkably short-sighted. You don't know what's good for you."

"Get out of my schoolroom this instant, you horrid monster! I won't!"

"A word with you in the passage, then," said the imperturbable Nelmont. His glance apparently conveyed some kind of warning to Donata; for she flounced out of the room, slamming the door after her. Elizabeth remained alone, angry and tearful.

Yesterday, it had seemed easy to have a quiet and gentle mind. To-day, it seemed impossible. In all her dreams of the future, she had included no such scene as this!

Chapter 3

MY SILKS AND FINE ARRAY

NELMONT'S "word" took twenty minutes to say. But when Donata Deveril came back to the schoolroom, Elizabeth was surprised to find that his arguments, whatever they were, had prevailed with his unruly cousin. Donata's manner had quite changed. She came forward, saying quietly:

"Will you forgive me, Miss Green? Until Nelmont lectured me in the passage I had no notion how detestably I had behaved. But you will agree that it would be a shock to any girl to find herself confronted with such a very young governess."

From being highly indignant, Elizabeth had fought her way back to calmness.

"It was a shock for me as well as for you," she said, with quivering lips. "I thought I should be teaching a little girl of six or seven——"

"Six or seven! What *can* my good cousin Mrs. Deveril have said in the letter to your Tadpole? Her wits must have gone completely astray."

"I did not hear the letter," said Elizabeth. "See, I brought my imaginary little girl this set of paper dolls, and I proposed to read these tales aloud in her playtime."

Donata looked and laughed. "Oh, what charming dollies!—the prettiest I have ever seen! I vow, they make me quite regret I am not six! And dear old *Jemima Placid* that I lost years ago when I lived with my grandmother, and mourned for with bitter tears! I must read *Jemima* again at once, for old times' sake. You do pardon me, Miss Green? You will stay?"

"My staying here will be useless," said Elizabeth. "What good can I do, if you are always to be feeling yourself the laughing-stock of the county?"

"Oh, but I have thought of a way out of that—such a clever way!" cried Donata eagerly. "Tell me, has anyone in the house seen you save Standing, Mrs. Hunt, and the schoolroom maid, Kitty? No? Now tell me, did they see you after or before you laid aside that enormous flapping black cloak in which you must surely look about five hundred years old?"

"Before. But how do you know I have a black cloak?"

"I peeped into your room," answered Donata, quite unabashed. "Well, if *they* don't know how extremely young you are, then nobody else need know either. You wouldn't object, would you, to dressing yourself to look a little older than you are?"

"No," said Elizabeth. "Miss Tadcaster recommended me always to choose sober colours and cuts when I buy clothes for myself; for a governess should always dress sedately, in advance of her age. But I cannot possibly buy any new clothes at present. Besides, two new dresses, one of thick stuff and one of thin, are always given to every girl on leaving Crowgarth's. I was measured and fitted for mine last night. They will be coming shortly by the carrier."

"Oh, we can't wait for them to arrive! No, I have a better proposal to make than that, a proposal that need not involve you in expense either. Two years ago a great-aunt bequeathed me a large part of her wardrobe. I don't know what use she thought a girl like me could make of an octogenarian's clothes!—but there they are, stuffed away in two big boxes in the attic! Nel and I have been routing about, and we have found apparel that will add half a century to your age. Come and see."

Elizabeth did not know whether to be pleased or offended. However, a pause for thought showed her that it was reasonable for Donata to wish to be taught by a governess who did not look as if she had that morning left the second class at Crowgarth's Female Orphanage. She could not entirely grasp the motives that had induced Mr. Nelmont Deveril to interest himself in the affairs of his cousin and his cousin's governess; but never having met him or any other boy before, she could only conclude that he was a scapegrace with a kind heart, who had used his influence to bring Donata to a better frame of mind.

"Very well," said the new governess, with what dignity she could call to her aid, "I will come."

"And as quickly as you can," said Donata; "for at any minute Cosmo may return home and wish to see you. He is in Falfont St. Philip this morning, but he will soon be back. You must be dressed before he appears."

They hastened to the attics, passing on the way Nel, comfortably ensconced in a window-seat. Donata led her victim into a lumber room. From the gaping mouths of two huge trunks rose a powerful aroma of moth-balls. Flung heedlessly down on the floor were old-fashioned gowns, shawls, tippets and cloaks of rich hues and costly materials.

"Great-Aunt Georgina was exactly your size—what a consummate piece of luck!" proclaimed Donata, measuring an armful of magenta silk against Elizabeth's slim length. "This might have been made for you."

Elizabeth donned the magenta gown, which did indeed fit her like a glove. From a cracked mirror on the wall, her brown eyes stared solemnly and strangely back at her. "I do look old—and queer!" she sighed as she pinned a lace cap with magenta bows on her curls.

"Yes, you might be a dowager," Donata agreed. "Now try on this violet, and the reseda, and the grey taffeta."

The magenta, the violet and their fellows were set aside for Sundays and festal occasions, and some sober browns and blacks were adjudged proper for everyday use.

"You might be Mrs. Hunt's double," said Donata, prancing round her sable-clad governess in delight; "you look fully as antiquated as she does! Here are a pair of green glasses for weak eyes—they will be a perfect finishing touch!"

"I will not wear green glasses," Elizabeth said firmly.

"I only thought," said Donata, "that they might distract Cosmo's attention from your cheek. Nel and I are not very anxious for him to find out that you were damaged in the catastrophe this morning. If you are set against wearing glasses, would you oblige us by putting on this furred cape with the high collar? It is the kind of thing my last-governess-but-two always wore when she was suffering from what she called *tic-doloureux* and other people called face-ache."

At this moment Nelmont tapped at the door.

"Cosmo wants to see us both, Donnet. It's about the coach business. Old Watson met him in Falfont St. Philip. He's waiting in the library."

"Miserable sneak!" said Donata, not explaining whether the designation was intended for her cousin or for Mr. Watson. She clattered after Nelmont.

Elizabeth carried her borrowed plumes downstairs and bestowed them in wardrobe and chest of drawers. The rest of the finery she re-packed in the two trunks, and then betook herself to the schoolroom to wait for the reappearance of her pupil. At the end of half an hour, Donata came leaping back, to find a pale, frightened governess.

"Such a blowing-up we got!" said Donata. "I think Cosmo used every term of abuse in the dictionary. Now he wants to see you, Miss Green. What's the matter? Why, I declare you're trembling! Did you think Cosmo had been pitching into us all this time? Not he!—he said all that he had to say in two minutes. Nel and I have been down at the stables ever since, leaving Cosmo to kick his heels in the library. I think perhaps you had better hurry, Miss Green. Cosmo has been waiting a tremendous time—and I have revenged myself famously for all the nasty things he said to me!"

Without waiting to ascertain the whereabouts of the library, Elizabeth hurried off at a pace unsuited to a discreet governess. In the great entrance hall, she tripped over her long skirt just as Mr. Cosmo Deveril, weary of waiting, sallied forth in search of Miss Green. He caught her and swung her to her feet.

"I beg your pardon, Sir!" cried Elizabeth in confusion. "Your message did not reach me as soon as it should have done. I was not aware that you were waiting——"

"Do not trouble to explain," said Mr. Cosmo. "I can well understand the reason for your delay."

He smiled at her. Elizabeth liked his smile.

"I ought to have known better than to entrust a message of importance to Donata immediately after she had received a rebuke, however well deserved! Even now, she has not conveyed it correctly. I desired her to ask when it would be convenient for you to receive me in the schoolroom. I did not request you to wait on me here. My mother and I are grateful to you for coming so promptly to take charge of our wild young cousin. May I beg you to spare me a few minutes?"

In the book-lined library they sat facing each other in two winged arm-chairs. The light from stained-glass windows fell on Elizabeth in moth-balled cape and black silk robe, and on Mr. Cosmo in dark green suit and white stock.

"I am afraid you may have some trouble with Donata," he said frankly. "As her recent escapade will have shown you, she is not easily controlled. In the few weeks since her arrival she has worn out the patience of an excellent daily governess well known to this family and much loved by them. Miss Berrington—I give you the lady's name because you are sure to hear it sooner or later—resigned her post at a moment's notice, in despair. I hope you will have an easier task. Both my mother and I have spoken seriously to Donata about her behaviour to Miss Berrington's successor. She has promised to reform, and I think she would keep her promise if my youngest brother did not happen, most unluckily, to be at home from school for a time, studying with a clerical tutor in the next village. It must be your endeavour, Miss Green, to keep the two apart, as far as you reasonably can. In the absence of boy companions of his own age, Nelmont has struck up a friendship with Donata that is not for the good of either of them."

"I do not see," said Elizabeth, "how I am to prevent them from speaking to each other."

"I am not asking you to anything quite so drastic," said Mr. Cosmo, smiling again. "I merely look to you to put a stop to the reckless adventures that will soon make Donata the talk of the neighbourhood. You would do us all an inestimable service if you could interest Donata in quiet, ladylike pursuits, such as needlework, pianoforte-playing, and—and—oh, well, looking after flowers and ferns and canaries and that sort of thing. You know what I mean."

Before Elizabeth's eyes rose a mental picture of Donata in her muddy riding-habit, thundering up the attic stairs with her tawny-yellow mane streaming down her back. The hope of interesting Donata in quiet, ladylike pursuits was faint indeed.

"I will do my best, Sir."

"My mother thought that perhaps some new lesson books might be useful in overcoming Donata's distaste for her studies. Miss Berrington insisted, perhaps unwisely, on keeping to the books she had used with my sister. Would you care to drive to Falfont St. Philip to-morrow for a consultation with our excellent bookseller, Mr. Leatherby? Pray order whatever you see fit."

"Thank you, Sir, I shall be glad to visit the bookshop."

"I have one small request to make, Miss Green. Will you very kindly escort Donata to Watermill Farm this afternoon before three o'clock, that she may apologize in person to Mr. Watson? I have told my brother that he must accompany me on a similar errand a little later."

"I will do so, Sir. And—and I will try hard to help Donata to become all that you and Mrs. Deveril can desire."

"Thank you, Miss Green. I feel sure that you will be as good as your word."

Cosmo rose to open the door for Elizabeth. She hoped that the upstanding fur collar had not knocked her cap askew; for she noticed that he was looking slightly beyond her instead of at her, in a way that was at once embarrassed and polite.

The schoolroom wing was very quiet when she came to it. Donata and Nelmont had been talking busily enough while she was leaving it; but they were not talking now. A frightful foreboding entered Elizabeth's heart as she neared the door panels. In a matter of seconds, the foreboding was justified. The cousins had vanished.

Chapter 4

A PATIENT MIND

"I WONDER," said Elizabeth to herself, "whether they have gone down to Watermill Farm *together* to apologize, instead of waiting to be taken there separately by Mr. Cosmo Deveril and me. I will go and find out."

She could have taken her choice of Great-Aunt Georgina's mantles; but she preferred to put on the black cloak that still linked her to Crowgarth's. Thus attired, she rang for Kitty and asked to be directed to Watermill Farm.

It was not far off, and Kitty's directions were clear. Once out of the park and into the highroad, Elizabeth followed a footpath that led her through meadows golden with buttercups to the farmhouse, where she was greeted by the farmer's kindly wife. Yes, said Mrs. Watson, Miss and Master Deveril had called, not long since. They did not say what their errand was, but told her they wanted to speak to her husband, who was down, as it happened, on the marshes. Would the young lady like to step in and rest herself till they came back? There was no use in going down to such a sad, dirty place to get one's shoes bogged in the mire.

As Great-Aunt Georgina's walking-shoes were of delicate kid intended for wear on the shortest of promenades round a London square, Elizabeth decided to accept the invitation. She and Mrs. Watson sat in the neat farm parlour, saying nothing. For the second time in a day Elizabeth felt that somebody was trying hard not to stare at her odd attire. It seemed to her that there could be no harm in telling this friendly woman, who was not a resident at the Court, that she was obliging Donata by wearing clothes fitter for a governess of respectable age.

"I am not as old as I look, Mrs. Watson," she began.

"No, Miss, I can see you are not," said Mrs. Watson, rather flustered.

"But I am dressed like this in order to add to my age. Miss Deveril feels—and I quite agree with her—that it is humiliating for her to be taught by a girl of her own age. There was a mistake about my coming. We think that in her anxiety about her sister's health, Mrs. Deveril forgot to ask for a governess in the thirties or forties from the register of past pupils. So I was sent instead, though I am only fifteen. I come from Crowgarth's Female Orphanage, and my name is Green."

Mrs. Watson started. Her pleasant face became quite grey, and she glanced quickly round with a furtive look.

"Crowgarth's? Oh, Miss Green, do you know anything of a little child called Isabella Marsh?"

"Tibbie Marsh? Oh, yes, I do! We elder girls were appointed 'school mothers' to the babies. Tibbie was one of mine. I loved her very much. Did you know her before she came to us?"

"I've never seen her. But her mother—I used to know her mother very well——" Mrs. Watson hesitated and then said in a rush: "I must speak, Miss Green, I can't keep it to myself. My daughter Mary disobeyed her father and me, and married a sorry scamp against our wishes. When she and her husband both died, his parents took charge of Isabella. I suppose they got tired of keeping her; for I've lately heard—the news was long in coming round—that they put her in the Orphanage last year. And Mr. Watson won't let me take her out and bring her home, nor even go to see her. He says that have anything to do with Rick Marsh's child he will not. He's a terrible obstinate man, my master. We've had more high words in the last six weeks than in all the twenty-eight years of our married life. Seems as if my whole mind is set on getting Isabella here as soon as ever I can. I don't give Watson a moment's peace."

Mrs. Watson no longer looked as bland and

mild as one of her own brown-velvety cows in the buttercup meadows. Her face was hard, red, angry as she said: "The good lady up at the Court—Mrs. Deveril—she tells me to pray. Pray, and be patient, she says. Who could be patient, situated like me? And as for praying—I'd be ashamed to trouble the Lord with mentioning quarrels between me and Mr. Watson. There isn't any warrant for it in the Bible."

Elizabeth thought: "How like Tibbie is to both her grandparents! She can be led, but she won't be driven. Oh, what can I say that would help Mrs. Watson to have a patient mind? I don't remember any Bible verses that exactly fit her very odd case. Unless perhaps part of Psalm Thirty-seven would *do*. It came into my mind this morning when I was beginning to feel angry and impatient with Nelmont and Donata . . . it's soothing."

"Was Mrs. Deveril thinking of the Thirty-seventh Psalm?" said Elizabeth aloud. "Under other names, it has some verses about patience. I can't say them by heart, but you could read them for yourself, couldn't you?"

The large Family Bible was on the moon-shaped yellow centre table, reposing on a mat of ruffled red wool. Elizabeth was taken aback when Mrs. Watson put the Book in front of her and asked her, civilly enough, to read the verses in question; for she herself had been crying so much lately that her eyes were in a poor way.

Elizabeth found the place and read:

> "Trust in the Lord, and do good; so shalt thou dwell in the land, and verily thou shalt be fed.
>
> Delight thyself also in the Lord; and He shall give thee the desires of thine heart.
>
> Commit thy way unto the Lord; trust also in Him, and He shall bring it to pass:
>
> And He shall bring forth thy righteousness as the light, and thy judgment as the noon-day.
>
> Rest in the Lord, and wait patiently for Him: fret not thyself because of him who prospereth in his way, because of the man that bringeth wicked devices to pass.
>
> Cease from anger, and forsake wrath: fret not thyself in any wise to do evil."

Elizabeth shut the Bible. She would have liked to tell Mrs. Watson of the help that the words had been to her only that morning; but speech stuck fast and would not come. So she said: "And now I'll tell you about little Tibbie, so that you can think about her while you are doing what the Psalmist tells us to do—trust, wait, and rest."

Mrs. Watson dried her eyes and listened. They were still talking about Tibbie when Farmer Watson was seen approaching with Nelmont and Donata. All three were cheerful, and Donata was laughing. Plainly, an armistice had been signed.

"Oh, there's my new governess!" cried Donata. "We've outwitted you and Cosmo, Miss Green! —we weren't going to be brought down like two babies, to say we were sorry! We've made peace independently, haven't we, Mr. Watson?"

"Aye, Missie," said the gruff farmer, who was surveying Elizabeth from top to toe in the greatest astonishment. Unlike his wife and his landlord, he did not attempt to avert his eyes. A prolonged stare followed the embarrassed Elizabeth half-way across the buttercup meadows.

"Phew!" said Donata. "Camphor! Those moth-balls must have been guaranteed to last for ever! A pity we hadn't an opportunity to air Great-Aunt Georgina's clothes before you put them on, Miss Green! I wonder whether the perfume staggered Cosmo as much as it appeared to stagger Mr. Watson. Do you think it will have worn off by dinner-time, Nel?"

"Doesn't matter if it hasn't," said Nel. "You won't be dining downstairs to-day—you and Miss Green will have your dinner served in the schoolroom. Cosmo's got friends coming."

Donata pranced indignantly.

"How stupid and fussy Cosmo is! Just because his mother is away from home, I'm to have tepid soup and congealed mutton in a poky schoolroom! And it isn't as if I had no governess to keep me in order. I declare I'll defy him and his edicts. We will march into the dining-room together, won't we, Miss Green?"

"Indeed we will not!" said Elizabeth. She remembered words spoken by Miss Tadcaster, and added like a dutiful parrot: "I could not countenance such improper behaviour."

Nel burst out laughing, then recovered himself and looked absurdly sober. Donata did not laugh. She sulked all the way home.

Chapter 5

SPORT FOR LADIES

ELIZABETH was not to learn what Mr. Cosmo Deveril thought of the audacious manner in which he and Miss Green had been tricked in their first attempt to break up the alliance between his brother and his cousin. He preserved, then and afterwards, a dignified silence on the subject. Nor did Elizabeth need to devise schemes for keeping her wilful pupil away from the dangerous Nel during the next few hours; for that young gentleman found the company in the dining-room so much more to his taste that he did not come near the school-room wing all the rest of the evening. Governess and pupil dined at five, Donata still sulking as she listened to distant sounds of talk and laughter.

The meal over, she resigned herself to her fate, and began to question Elizabeth about life at Crowgarth. Indifferent at first, she soon became eager to hear more, and turned a deaf ear to Elizabeth's timid suggestions that they should make ready for the studies of the next day. "What's the use?" she asked impatiently. "Aren't we going to Falfont St. Philip in the morning to buy new books to replace the antique horrors dear to Miss Berrington's heart? Go on, do! Did you ever have a midnight feast at Crowgarth's? Was there a school ghost? Which of your 'babies' did you like best?"

"I tried not to make favourites," Elizabeth answered. "But I think I really loved Tibbie Marsh the most."

"I know something about the girl called Marsh," said Donata. "Cousin Mildred—Mrs. Deveril, you know—was telling Cosmo what Mrs. Watson told her, about Marsh's being a grandchild, and how Farmer Watson was behaving like the fattest and squealiest and contrariest of all his pigs. They—Cousin Mildred and Cosmo, not the pigs—seemed very sorry for Mrs. Watson. Did she talk to you about little Marsh? She looked as though she had been crying."

"Yes, Mrs. Watson told me."

"And what did you say?"

"I read her some verses out of a Psalm."

"You *what*? You read the Bible to her? How very odd!"

"I do not see that it was odd. If we may not read the Bible when we are perplexed or distressed, when may we read it?"

Donata had nothing to say to that. She asked curiously:

"What Psalm did you read?"

There was a Bible on the shelves. Elizabeth found the place and gave the Book to Donata, who shook her golden mane all over her shoulders before reading the passage under its cover.

"Well," she said at last, "I'm sure it's very excellent advice and all that, but it wouldn't have suited me one tiny scrap if I had been Mrs. Watson. I should have wanted to be told that I was quite justified in going to the Orphanage, taking my grandchild out, bringing her home, and snapping my fingers at Mr. Watson! I like having my own way about everything . . . Now, have you any more stories about the orphan who crept into the larder to steal Miss Tadcaster's blackberry pie and cream? What became of her in the end?"

Elizabeth related Crowgarthian life-histories until she grew tired. "It's your turn to talk," she said at last. "Pray let me hear a little about you."

"You've heard it," said Donata, with a shrug of the shoulders.

"No, I have not. Mrs. Deveril only said——"

"That I was as unmanageable as an unbroken colt and as ignorant as a donkey?"

"Well, not in those words," said Elizabeth cautiously.

"I thought so! But didn't she say anything else?"

"No, I believe not. Except, of course, that you had lately come to live at the Court."

"You were told that I lived with my grandmother at first? And that I was later transferred to an aunt's house, that I 'might enjoy the benefits of youthful companionship'? Now

I'm here. You needn't ask me any more; for I don't intend to tell you another word."

The room became very quiet. Elizabeth knew then that there was some mystery connected with Donata's coming to the Court.

"But I don't mind telling you why Nel is here," said Donata, raising her head to show a sudden wicked sparkle in her eyes. "He ought to be at Eton. But he has been so daring and lazy and turbulent that his guardians took him away for a time, as a punishment. Cosmo and Ughtred didn't approve of the guardians' action, nor did Cousin Mildred; but their protests were disregarded. The guardians say that it depends entirely on Nel himself whether he goes back at the beginning of the next half year—or ever! It will be never, I think. He does less work for his tutor than he did at Eton, and Cosmo and Ughtred say it takes them all their time to keep him out of mischief. Since I came, Nel has been worse, much worse."

"You ought not to boast of it!" cried Elizabeth, horrified. "It is woman's place to encourage man in all that is good."

"Spake Miss Tadcaster! How Nel would laugh if I tried to improve his morals! I live in a glass house, Miss Green, so I can't enjoy the pleasure of throwing stones. Don't look so horribly shocked! Nel is a madcap, a scatter-brain, an idler—and I am all that and more too. I am not saying this to frighten you away, mind! When I first saw you, that's what I meant to do; but I don't propose to do it now. For one thing, Nel has advised me against it, quite seriously. For another, I like you. I don't know why I should; for as a rule I don't get on with girls. In Aunt Hester and Uncle Charles's house I hated all my cousins except the two boys, Harry and Peregrine. You're an oddity, but you are an improvement on the girlkind I've met so far. Where is your *Jemima Placid* that you were going to read to the sweet little niminy-piminy maiden who doesn't exist? As Nel isn't here to laugh, pray read it to me!"

"Very well, if you will fetch your needlework," said Elizabeth.

"My needlework? I used it as a towel to dry Nel's dog when he fell into the green, slimy pond last week. I haven't seen it since."

The next morning Mr. Cosmo Deveril accompanied his cousin and his cousin's governess to Falfont St. Philip where, in the middle of a busy morning's shopping, he treated them to hot chocolate and cheesecakes in the pastry-cook's parlour. Donata saw nothing particularly delightful in hours spent over the choice of lesson books, improved globes, drawing and sewing materials; but it was a radiant face that peeped out of the depths of Great-Aunt Georgina's purple straw poke bonnet. Elizabeth enjoyed that expedition to the full. Never before had she been at liberty to buy as many books as she wanted, both for her own use and Donata's, and never before had she owned a whole guinea to be hoarded or expended as she pleased. She looked forward eagerly to an afternoon of unpacking and arranging, with a pleasant evening walk when all was done.

Alas for her bright anticipations! On their return Kitty handed a note to Donata, who went with it to her own room and thereafter disappeared. Inquiries were fruitless: nobody knew what had become of the young lady. Consulted, Mrs. Hunt failed to give the promised help. Nel, she announced despairingly, had fifty chosen friends and as many ways, mostly disreputable, of spending his time. He might have taken Donata otter-hunting, eel-spearing, fair-gazing, clay-pigeon shooting, what you please. It was to be hoped that he had not taken her to a rat-catching. Mr. Cosmo Deveril would put up with many of Miss Donata's freaks, but not with that!

"Do you know," Elizabeth asked, "where rats are likely to be caught?"

Mrs. Hunt was offended by the supposition that she had any knowledge whatever of such proceedings. There were, she assured Elizabeth, a very large number of farms and private grounds infested by rats. Miss Green might as well spare herself the trouble of going in pursuit of Donata. It was a hundred chances to one that her steps would direct themselves to the right spot.

Turning disconsolately away, Elizabeth met Kitty waiting out of sight.

"I don't know for sure, Miss Green," Kitty whispered, "but I think I may be right in mentioning that the rat-hunt is likelier than not to be at Falfont Manor. Only, whatever happens, don't let Mr. Nel and Miss Donnet know I told you. My life won't be worth living if you do, Miss."

Elizabeth gladly promised silence and hurried off on the long walk to Falfont Manor. Yells and shouts from the Manor stableyard told her that the hunt was up. She opened a door in the wall and fell back screaming into a currant bush as a huge rat flew past her down the path, pursued by a dozen boys and a girl with floating golden hair.

"Donata!" said Elizabeth from the middle of the currant bush, "you will come home with me at once! This is not sport for ladies."

"I'm not coming!" said Donata, thumping the ground wrathfully with her stick. "If it isn't just like you to turn up here, spoiling all my fun!"

Her eyes still tightly shut for fear of horrible sights, Elizabeth scrambled out of the bush and said, steadily but with sinking heart: "Very well then, I must tell Mr. Deveril that I resign my post. If I am unable to control you, I am not justified in continuing to call myself your governess."

"You composed that fine sentence beforehand," said Donata, glowering and thumping harder than ever. "Are you in earnest? You won't like slinking home a failure in only two days! Yesterday you were ready to cry at the thought of it."

"I mean what I say."

"Oh, all right, then! Wait here while I get my pony, you interfering old——"

The rest of the sentence was lost in dark mutterings that Elizabeth tried not to hear. They paced home in gloomy silence, Donata leading the pony.

Once more in the schoolroom, Donata flung herself into a chair.

"I am not going to listen to a lecture," she announced. "There's nothing to lecture me about. Nobody ever forbade me to take part in a rat-hunt, so I have done nothing wrong. When you told me to come home, I obeyed you at once. I have given no trouble at all."

Elizabeth felt that there was a flaw somewhere in Donata's arguments, though she could not detect it. She remained silent.

"Oh, how tired I am!" complained Donata, with an enormous yawn. "I hate walking on rough roads!—but I suppose I shall hardly ever be able to ride again, except at the cost of a quarrel with you."

"If——" began Elizabeth.

"If—what?"

"Nothing. I changed my mind about speaking."

"I know! You were going to say 'If I

learnt to ride?' It's a very good thought. Nel and I will teach you."

Shuddering, Elizabeth agreed.

Mr. Cosmo Deveril had no dinner-guests that day. At the family table, Donata announced, with much laughter, that Miss Green had promised to take riding-lessons. Resplendent in ivory and subfusc satin cap and gown, the governess meekly answered "No, Sir," to Cosmo's courteous "I hope Donata has not worried you into consenting, Miss Green? You are not afraid that the exercise will be too strenuous for you?"

"Oh, we won't teach her to jump hedges or anything risky, will we, Nel?" said Donata. "As you say, Cosmo, it wouldn't be advisable, at her advanced age."

"Donata!" said Cosmo, in horror.

Elizabeth did not fathom the swift flash of amusement that passed between Nel and his cousin. Then Donata said carelessly: "Oh, Miss Green understands me! It's just my rattling way. She won't take offence."

There was nothing to take offence at, as far as Elizabeth could see. The words, slighting if applied to an elderly woman, were harmless enough when directed at a youthful governess who was trying to look older than her years.

"We thought that Miss Green would feel safe on Snowball," Donata added. "Snowball is sure-footed, though rather slow. You agree, do you not, Cosmo?"

"An excellent choice," said Cosmo.

Snowball was an aged white mare, long since retired from duty, who rambled at will in the park. The next morning, after their studies were over, the cousins gave Elizabeth her first riding-lesson, in the course of which Donata pointed with her switch to a house in a grove of trees.

"That is where Mrs. Vallard lives. She is an old friend of Cousin Mildred, and Nel's godmother. She's blind, poor unfortunate. Before you came, Cousin Mildred arranged that from next Sunday onwards I should spend Sunday and Wednesday afternoons and evenings at Beech Grove, so that you might have some time to yourself. Nel comes too, quite often. He's rather fond of his godmother. We are both perfectly good and sober while we are in her house—we behave as stolidly as the china figures on her mantelpiece. But perhaps Cosmo has told you this already?"

"Mrs. Hunt has mentioned it," said Elizabeth.

She was secretly glad to know that for a few short hours in each week, somebody else would be wholly responsible for Donata. When Sunday afternoon came, she sighed with relief as she parted from her pupil at Mrs. Vallard's gate after Evening Prayer, which was said early in the afternoon in the little church at the end of the park. It was refreshing to feel that from then till bedtime, her burden was laid down.

Chapter 6

ENTRY IN A THOUGHT BOOK

DEVERIL COURT was very quiet on that summer Sunday. Following his usual observance, Mr. Cosmo Deveril had ridden into Falfont St. Philip to visit his maternal grandparents, and Nel was presumably either with his brother or with his own friends or engaged in taking tea with Donata in his blind godmother's house. Elizabeth felt at liberty to wander where she would in garden and park, thinking about the past and the future.

Those first days had been, on the whole, satisfactory. She had received a notably kind letter from Mrs. Deveril, which she had answered in the most elegant language at her command and in the handwriting that was, as Donata remarked with satisfaction, "so much more like an old lady's than a girl's". Nor had Donata given as much trouble as her loving relatives had feared. She had been exceedingly idle over her lessons with Elizabeth and over her preparation for the visiting masters; but she had not been insolent or defiant, nor had she seen more of wild Nel than his mother and brother would deem "reasonable". Elizabeth had the satisfaction of knowing that it was likely she would see even less of him in the near future. When Mr. Ughtred Deveril came down from Oxford for the Long Vacation, all three brothers were going to be very busy in promoting the election of a friend who was standing for Parliament.

There was, however, one factor that had not entered Elizabeth's calculations when she set out on her journey to Deveril Court; it had not then occurred to her that she might have to take pains to keep up with her pupil. Donata was backward, but she was clever and argumentative. Elizabeth already began to entertain a suspicion that if Donata had been a diligent member of the second class at Crowgarth's, the six talented young persons of quite extraordinary gifts might have trembled for their places. A governess of less exalted capacity would certainly have to work hard for her living. But this was a vexatious thought that could be kept for weekday contemplation. On this sunny day of rest she had other matters to think about.

As she paced the rose garden, Elizabeth was planning what she should put in a stout manuscript book that she had purchased at the bookshop in Falfont St. Philip for use as a thought book. All the elder girls at Crowgarth kept "thought books"; it was a recently established fashion, which Elizabeth meant now to follow.

An hour later, she laid down her pen on the entrance of Kitty with her tea.

"La, Miss, how well you do write!" said the maid, with a little sound of envy in her voice. "I tell Miss Donata I wish I'd had her chances when I was a child."

"Can't you write, Kitty?"

"No, nor read neither. Never had any schooling. I was left an orphan, handed round among my relations like a parcel. Nobody cared."

Elizabeth felt a thrill of sympathy. "I am an orphan too."

"Are you, Miss? Well, to be sure!"

"Would you like to learn to read and write, Kitty?"

"That I would, Miss. You see, it never mattered till I came here. But the servants at Deveril Court are so highly educated that I'm ashamed for them to know how ignorant I am. There they sit of a Sunday afternoon, reading their books by the hour together. I have to sit too, turning the pages over and pretending to read till I get the cramp cruel."

Elizabeth was thinking. Should she offer to teach Kitty? To do so would be to lose some of the precious hours that she wanted for herself.

Then she caught sight of a line she had just transcribed:

"Jesu's is a *loving* mind."

That settled the question. One couldn't truthfully pray "Plant, and root, and fix in me All the mind that was in Thee" when one was refusing to give up a little bit of time.

"Kitty, you ought to learn to read. If you don't, you won't be able ever to read the Bible to yourself."

"That's true, Miss. I have a Bible, too. Mrs. Deveril, she gave me one—such a beauty!"

"I could teach you to read and write, if you could come here on Wednesdays and Sundays."

Kitty's face wore a broad smile of delight.

"That I can, Miss."

So after tea, Elizabeth resolutely postponed the browsing she had promised herself in the bookshelves, and gave her full attention to instructing Kitty in two of the three R's.

Kitty was an apt and diligent pupil, who was only too glad to slip into her pocket the child's reading book that had been the first prize Elizabeth ever received. When the maid went out, Donata came in, pettishly, with clouded brow.

She threw herself into a chair and said sulkily: "I've come home early. Something annoyed me."

"You did not return unaccompanied, I trust," said Elizabeth, mindful of her duty as a governess.

"No, Nel came with me."

The mention of Nel's name brought a darker

cloud. Donata was silent for a time. Recovering herself, she looked about in search of pastime. Her glance fell on the manuscript book.

"What's that? A diary? Do you keep a diary and write verses, Miss Green? How delicious!"

"It is a 'thought book'," Elizabeth explained. "But I have not got to writing down any of my own thoughts yet."

"If it's only quotations, may I look?"

Barely waiting for permission, Donata took up the book. Her eyes grew large and round.

"Very suitable for Sunday!" she said. "A text, a hymn, and a prayer! But what a queer hymn! Why did you write it down? It doesn't seem to me to be very good poetry."

"It may not be very good poetry, but it is very good truth," said Elizabeth. "It was the hymn we sang on my last morning at Crowgarth's. The text is my 'leaving text' given me by Miss Tadcaster, to carry into the world with me. I chose the collect because it fitted in so perfectly with the hymn and the text:

> "Grant, we beseech Thee, merciful Lord, to Thy faithful people pardon and peace; that they may be cleansed from all their sins, and serve Thee with a quiet mind; through Jesus Christ our Lord."

Donata stood playing with the leaves of the book.

"I presume you are what is called religious," she said. "I have never had a genuinely religious governess, save Miss Berrington, who was with me such a short time that she doesn't really count. With my other governesses, religion was just a glossy sort of pretence. I can see that it isn't a pretence with you. So I think I will tell you something that explains why I am annoyed. Nobody in this house knows it except Cousin Mildred. She did say she thought my governess ought to be told; but I begged and implored till she promised not to speak. But now it's no use trying to hide the secret any longer. Everybody will know soon."

Turning one shoulder on Elizabeth, she said: "I told you I did not like my girl cousins. Rhoda was the most hateful. She was the eldest, quite grown up. I couldn't bear her. Once, to pay her out for her general hatefulness, I wrote a make-believe love-letter from her to a young man named George Willoughby, whom I knew she liked, though he didn't care a rap for her."

"A—a *love-letter?*" gasped Elizabeth. "You cannot mean it? You never could have done such a wicked, wicked deed."

"Oh yes, I did!" Donata answered jauntily. "Rhoda was perpetually borrowing novels from the circulating library. I copied out a letter in which the dashing Lady Eglantyne Montmorency sent Lord Algernon Villiers a rosebud and a spray of forget-me-not. I sent the letter off in such a temper that I never stopped to consider the consequences. As soon as I cooled down, I saw how insanely I had behaved. But, before I had a chance to write to George Willoughby and beg him to overlook the foolish joke I had played on him—before I could do it, the worst had happened. He came to see Rhoda's father, my Uncle Charles Ponsonby."

Elizabeth was white with horror. "And then——?" she whispered.

"He came to apologize for having, as he thought, unintentionally caused Rhoda to misunderstand the nature of his feelings towards her. Oh, he was exceedingly concerned, the stupid, stupid owl! You needn't frown, Miss Green. Truly, he was the stupidest owl on the face of the globe. Stupid for not having guessed that somebody had played a trick on him and Rhoda, stupider for coming to apologize for what wasn't his fault, and stupidest for being all the time engaged to be married to somebody else, so that the affair could never be put straight after all! Well, Rhoda came into the room while her father was listening to Mr. Willoughby, insisted on hearing what was in dispute between them, asked to be allowed to look at the letter, recognized my handwriting, shrieked, and swooned away. I can tell you Uncle Charles and Aunt Hester sent me packing as soon as they had found a relative who would consent to house me. They would have sent me to a hideously strict boarding school if Rhoda hadn't, quite mistakenly, supposed that I should be worse off buried alive in the heart of the country with a widowed lady of strict religious principles. She over-reached herself finely! The Deverils are relations on my father's side and distant at that, so neither Rhoda nor Uncle and Aunt Hester had any notion that I should be coming to a happy home with one boy cousin, two men cousins and their delightful mother, who has been kinder to me than anyone ever was before, in spite of knowing what she does know."

"I can't tell what to say," said Elizabeth. "I never heard such a terrible story in my life."

"I don't suppose you ever did, living in an orphanage of tame white kittens," said Donata sombrely. "I'll admit that I was crazy to have done such a thing. Not that I care two straws about Rhoda's feelings!—but I do care for the consequences! Some of her friends have come to live here. With the whole of the United Kingdom to choose from, they must needs establish themselves in Falfont St. Philip! I met the Thompsons to-night, and they looked straight over my head, or through it, I don't know which. Their upthrust noses told me that piece of my wrong-doing will be round Falfont St. Philip like wildfire. Cosmo will be horrified beyond words. When Ughtred comes down from Oxford all proper and precise, he will hardly condescend to speak to me; and as for Nel—well, it won't ever be the same again after Nel knows, as know he soon will. Not that he will throw stones. As I told you before, he lives in a glass house himself. But it isn't the same kind of glass house, worse luck! Nel would have cut off his hand rather than do what I did."

Chapter 7

QUIETLY AND SABBATICALLY

DONATA sat silent, glumly regarding her shoes. When Elizabeth could speak for shame and dismay, she said: "If you have not done so already, you ought to tell your cousin, Miss Ponsonby, that you are sorry."

"Shan't. Not sorry. She got what she deserved. I'm only sorry for myself. This is what Nel calls 'coming a terrible cropper!'—just when I had made such plans for the future! And when I was having a most enjoyable evening, too!"

"I thought you did not greatly enjoy visiting your cousin's godmother?"

For some reason, Donata stammered slightly as she said:

"I don't, as a rule. But I enjoyed myself to-night. Oh dear, what a plague everything is! *You* never would have got yourself into such a fix, Miss Green. Being religious must be a help. Tell me, when did you start?"

"When did I start what?"

"Oh, you know! Loving God and your neighbour and doing all that the *Catechism* tells us to do! Everything I don't do, in short.

For I don't, you know. I attend church either because I'm obliged to attend or because I want to please a kind person like Cousin Mildred. I am accustomed to read the Psalms and Lessons with my successive governesses simply because all but you and old Berrington have considered that as much a mechanical part of school work as learning the pence table. You and she—yes, she too, in spite of her fiery-dragon temper!—are exceptions. There's a Chinese proverb that says 'a journey of a thousand miles begins with one step'. What was your first step?"

In Miss Tadcaster's garden at Crowgarth there had been clumps of striped green-and-cream ribbon grass, which the little ones had been allowed to pick to make sashes for their dolls. Long ago Elizabeth had often tried to find two blades striped exactly alike; but she never could. Always there was a delicate difference; it would seem that God cared for the grace of the fashioning of each leaf. Elizabeth found herself thinking of the ribbon grass as she prepared to answer Donata's question. Her own first step had been taken in ribbon-grass days, so early that she could hardly remember it and could not be sure that there had not been other steps before it. She knew only that, far in the past she had stood at the dormitory window, looking out at the starlit sky and singing to herself the verse that had puzzled Tibbie Marsh:

"Loving Jesu, gentle Lamb,
In Thy gracious hands I am!"

when suddenly the second line became alive with a meaning it had never had before. How the silver stars had glittered with unearthly splendour as she sang again and again, in awe and wonder: "In Thy gracious hands *I am*!"

But the first step had been different for every one of the dead Christians whose memoirs were in the Crowgarth library, and for the living Christians she had met. God's ways of dealing with human souls were as varied as His ways of colouring ribbon grass. Donata's first step would be different too.

"I am not sure that hearing about my 'first step' would necessarily help anybody else. You see, it was only a baby's step," said Elizabeth to Donata, apologetically. "But if you wish, I will tell you what it was."

She told. Donata said:

"I suppose that, or something like it, is how it ought to be. All I can say is, it has never happened to Donnet Deveril. And isn't it strange? With a dead father and a living mother and brothers as good and Christian as they could be, it has never happened—I am convinced it hasn't—to Nel. Of course, sometimes I have had serious thoughts, and so, I suppose, has he. But they have never come to anything, and we have both gone on walking in the wrong direction. Walking, did I say?

I ought to have said leaping, dancing, running! Your text and hymn and prayer are perfectly suitable for you because they are meant for one who has already set off in the right direction—but they are none of them applicable to poor Nel and me. If you had been choosing for me instead of yourself, what text and hymn and prayer would you have written down in your book?"

"I shall have to consider that carefully," said Elizabeth.

She felt ashamed of herself for failing to answer Donata's question as promptly and explicitly as no doubt Miss Tadcaster would have answered it, or Mrs. Deveril or Nel's godmother, Mrs. Vallard. But she gathered together enough courage to say:

"While I am thinking, couldn't you be writing to your Cousin Rhoda? You have used her very ill, you know you have. If you told her you were sorry for what you did, I do believe you would find it easier to—to turn round and walk in the right direction."

"Can't be done!" said Donata, firmly. "I fancy I hear Nel coming, Miss Green. Now don't say, as Miss Berrington did, that Nel ought not to haunt the schoolroom. He is going to employ his time usefully in picking the lock of the bottom drawer in your bureau—the drawer for which no key can be found. I am positively devoured with curiosity to discover what is inside. Miss Berrington was curious too; she said the drawer was always left empty in her years at the Court, as she never had occasion to use it. She thinks it must have been locked by a temporary governess who took charge of the former Miss Deveril when she, Miss Berrington, was ill."

"Picking locks is not a profitable occupation for Sunday evening," said Elizabeth, "nor do I need to have the drawer opened at present, since, like Miss Berrington, I have nothing to put in it. And as the bureau is Mr. Cosmo's property, he ought to be consulted before it is damaged in any way."

"Of all the prim fuss-makers!" said Donata. "Very well, I will employ myself quietly and sabbatically in some other way. Have I your leave to go down to Mrs. Hunt's sitting-room for an hour? I can't possibly get into mischief in her company."

She flew off without waiting for an answer.

Elizabeth spent some time in choosing a text, a hymn and a prayer that might be helpful to the Deveril cousins. At last she took a sheet of paper and wrote down the passages of her choice.

> "Grace be to you and peace from God the Father, and from our Lord Jesus Christ, Who gave Himself for our sins, that He might deliver us from this present evil world, according to the will of God and our Father: To whom be glory for ever and ever. Amen.

Jesus, Thou art our King!
To me Thy succour bring;
Christ, the mighty One, art Thou,
Help for all on Thee is laid;
This the word; I claim it now,
Send me now the promised aid.

High on Thy Father's throne,
O look with pity down!
Help, O help, attend my call,
Captive lead captivity:
King of glory, Lord of all,
Christ, be Lord, be King to me!

Almighty God, who hast given Thine only Son to be unto us both a sacrifice for sin, and also an ensample of godly life: Give us grace that we may always most thankfully receive that His inestimable benefit, and also daily endeavour ourselves to follow the blessed steps of His most holy life; through the same Jesus Christ our Lord. Amen."

After more thought, she wrote:

"The verses from the first chapter of the Epistle to the Galatians tell us about the 'inestimable benefit' that our Lord Jesus Christ conferred on us when He 'gave Himself for our sins'.

The hymn puts into our mouths the prayer of any person who is making for himself or herself the 'first step' in a journey of a thousand miles.

The collect is a prayer for every day of our journey after the first step."

Elizabeth left the sheet to dry, and busied herself with putting away Bible, Prayer Book, and hymn book. She was surprised and puzzled to find that her thought book was missing. Not without an uneasy suspicion as to what might have become of it, she went to discover what quiet sabbatical occupation Miss Donata Deveril was pursuing in Mrs. Hunt's parlour.

The door was ajar.

Sounds of very odd singing greeted Elizabeth's ears as she came down the passage. Drawing nearer, she heard Donata's voice raised in a loud nasal whine. Then Nel spoke, apparently in remonstrance. Donata broke off to say petulantly: "No, no, you shan't stop me! I'm going on to the end. Mrs. Hunt's enjoying it, aren't you, Mrs. Hunt?" And once more the twanging song began, bearing with it the words of Elizabeth's own treasured "leaving hymn".

"Hold your tongue, will you, Donnet?" Nel shouted. "I've had enough of this! I'm off."

"You'd better go to the schoolroom," Donata said tauntingly, "to learn how Christianity is like a journey of a thousand miles that begins with one step. She's there, writing piousities that she thinks may do good to our souls, yours and mine. I asked her to do it—ha, ha, ha! Oh, yow-w-w! Let go, you horrid ruffian, you shan't have it, I haven't finished—ow-w-w! you savage!"

Standing petrified at the angle of the passage, Elizabeth saw Nel burst out of the parlour, clutching her thought book. Donata charged after him. They dashed past Elizabeth without seeing her, rushed into the entrance hall—and stopped short, grave and demure in a second, at sight of a sedate young man by the hatstand.

Mr. Cosmo Deveril had returned home.

The schoolroom wing could be reached by way of the back stairs as well as the front. Elizabeth ran faster than she had ever run in her life, in the hope of reaching the shelter of her own room without meeting Nel or the treacherous Donata.

Behind her locked door she wept for mortification. The only drop of comfort in her bitter cup was the certainty that her presence in the passage had gone unnoticed: the young Deverils did not suspect that she had heard part of Donata's performance. But the comfort was poor, at best. How could she have been so foolish, she asked herself, as to be deceived by Donata's pretended earnestness? How could she?—how could she?

The frantic flight through the house had been, it appeared, unnecessary; for nothing was heard of the cousins. If Donata had resumed the quarrel and the chase after the meeting with Cosmo, she and Nel had doubtless betaken themselves to the park, where they could settle their dispute without interruption.

Elizabeth had stopped crying by the time the Sunday supper-bell rang; but her eyes were still so red that she was glad to hide them behind Great-Aunt Georgina's hitherto unused green spectacles, which were reposing in the top drawer of the schoolroom bureau. She went to find them.

Lying on the table as if it had never left its place was the thought book. The sheet of paper was no longer there.

The silent restoration of the one and removal of the other went some way towards indicating that Donata had come to her senses, outwardly at least.

"But I can't say any more about the paper, now that I know she didn't really want it," Elizabeth decided sadly. "I should have liked to do some extra explaining . . . but what I wrote is no use ever again. . . ."

The first glance from behind the dark glasses revealed to Elizabeth that either Nel or her own conscience had made Donata heartily ashamed of herself. Both she and Nel were so distant with each other and so civil to Miss Green that more than once Elizabeth saw Cosmo's eyebrows lifting themselves in surprise.

Donata's unusual courtesy was maintained throughout the rest of the evening. Elizabeth could well understand the guilty feelings that prompted what would otherwise have been a failure of politeness, namely, her singular omission to thank her governess for the trouble taken in writing out text, hymn and prayer. When they parted for the night, Donata paused as if about to ask a question; but she did not ask it.

"Good night, Miss Green," she said, and that was all.

Chapter 8

VIOLETS IN THE GRASS

ELIZABETH lay in a heap at the roadside, looking up at Snowball, who stood patiently by with an air of mild surprise on her long face. Neither of them could guess how it came about that Elizabeth had been thrown.

"One moment I was riding quietly along, and the next moment here I am!" said Elizabeth, lifting herself cautiously in an attempt to find out how many bones were broken. She was relieved to learn that all her limbs were intact, though she felt too giddy to rise. Lying still, she peered about in search of her companions. As she had expected, they were two small galloping dots half-way to the blue woods on the horizon.

Her situation might have been worse. She was reclining on a grassy bank that smelt sweetly of violets escaped from a garden. The garden itself was not far to seek, being on the opposite side of the lane. Over its fence peeped the shaggy head and twinkling eyes of a thatched cottage with glittering diamond-paned windows. The door of the cottage swung back, and a little old lady hurried down the path with such alarm in her face that Elizabeth scrambled hurriedly to her feet in reassurance. The world promptly began to spin round so fast that she was obliged to cling to Snowball until it steadied again.

"Come and rest, my child," said the old lady, fluttering about Elizabeth like a mother bird. "Surely you were not alone?"

Great-Aunt Georgina's feathered beaver riding-hat had fallen back from Elizabeth's curls. She was not surprised, therefore, to hear herself addressed as "child".

"No," she answered, "I am not alone. But I am such an inexperienced rider that the others found jogging along beside me unbearably slow. They rode ahead, across the common."

"They ought not to have left you," said the old lady indignantly.

"Oh, I have had several riding-lessons!" said Elizabeth. "They thought I was safe enough—and until five minutes ago, so did I! Thank you, Madam, I should be happy to sit in your parlour till they turn back to see what has become of me."

Elizabeth tethered Snowball to the fence and accompanied the old lady into a plain, neat parlour with a sofa drawn up beneath the window. Taking a pheasant-feather fan from the mantelpiece, the old lady fanned her invalid diligently. Elizabeth noticed that pheasant feathers, elaborately interwoven, formed the panels of a screen at the far side of the room.

Placidly tended by her hostess, Elizabeth rested until the effects of her fall passed off. Presently she sat up, refreshed.

"I cannot think," she said, "why the other two have not come back. It is odd."

"Very odd," agreed the old lady. "May I ask whom I have the pleasure of addressing?"

Elizabeth gave her name, and added that for nearly three weeks she had been the governess at Deveril Court.

"Ah!" said the old lady, with something like a sigh. "My name is Berrington, Mrs. Berrington. Perhaps you have heard my daughter's name mentioned by your pupil?"

"Miss Berrington? Oh, yes!" said Elizabeth.

She scolded herself for feeling hot and uncomfortable over the discovery that she had been thrown, as it were, into the house of the one whose place she had taken at the Court. But she could not drive away a sense of guilt, however often she recalled to memory the fact that Miss Berrington had thrown up her post of her own free will.

"Donata says that I am not nearly such a good teacher as Miss Berrington," Elizabeth ventured to say, after casting about for words that should mollify the hearer.

The statement was well received.

"Does she?" said Mrs. Berrington, with a

little pink glow in her withered cheek. "I am glad to hear it. There was a time when Miss Donata Deveril thought otherwise."

"She has learnt wisdom since then," said Elizabeth. "She tells me frankly that I have not the same knack of making my lessons entertaining, and that my explanations are confused instead of being, like Miss Berrington's, crystal clear."

Mrs. Berrington was plainly gratified by the tribute to her daughter; but she only said: "Time will mend all that, my dear. You are young."

"I am very young," said Elizabeth. "It is a pity."

The old face expressed such kindly sympathy that Elizabeth was encouraged to speak first of her life at Crowgarth and then of her experiences at Deveril Court. An account of her meeting with Tibbie Marsh's kinsfolk was interrupted by the sudden entrance of a tall gaunt woman of middle age, whom Elizabeth had seen at a distance in church, passing the Court pew always with averted auburn head.

Putting down the heavy basket of fir cones that she carried, the new-comer stood looking at the guest with unfriendly red-brown eyes. As soon as Mrs. Berrington had made them acquainted with each other, Elizabeth overcome with shyness, professed herself ready to ride home.

"Alone?—after a fall? Pray don't do anything

so foolish. You had better wait here till someone comes to look for you," said Miss Berrington ungraciously, after she had listened with barely concealed impatience to her mother's brief history of the accident. "What can Nelmont Deveril be about? He ought to have come in search of you long since. Sit down till his lordship chooses to put in an appearance."

Her manner was so authoritative that Elizabeth sank from governess to pupil in the space of a second. Much to her self-disgust, she knew that it would be easier to fly than to leave the sofa in defiance of Miss Berrington's command.

"My dear Miss Green," said Mrs. Berrington gently, "you really must not think of finding your way back to the Court by yourself. You will take tea with us, I trust, while you are waiting. Nelmont and his cousin will no doubt arrive shortly."

Miss Berrington did not support the invitation to take tea, but she strode from the room to make preparations in the kitchen that adjoined it.

"You were telling me about Mrs. Watson's distress over the little girl Tibbie Marsh," said the old lady, turning to Elizabeth. "I heard the story from Mrs. Watson herself, when she came to bring my daughter a setting of eggs for our black hen. My dear, I am so glad that you were able to show her where to look for comfort in her trouble. So many, alas, do not understand that the secret of life's happiness lies in the taking of Psalm Thirty-seven into our heart of hearts. But you will pardon me for saying that you are very young to have learnt from your own experience what it means to rest in the Lord, to wait patiently for Him, to delight in Him, to commit your way unto Him, to trust Him, and not to fret yourself in any wise to do evil."

"I am not sure that I do know what it means in the big things of life," said Elizabeth humbly. "In the little things, yes; but where important decisions are to be made, no. Perhaps it was presumptuous of me to offer any advice to someone so much older than I am, who was undergoing a great trial; but I was so sorry for Mrs. Watson that I couldn't help telling her of the words that had helped me in a little trial."

Mrs. Berrington said quietly: "It can never be presumptuous to remind a fellow-sufferer that 'in returning and rest shall ye be saved; in quietness and in confidence shall be your strength'. My long life has shown me that the troubles even of Christian people are caused by their relying on their own strength, putting their trust in themselves, and choosing their own way."

While she listened, Elizabeth's thoughts strayed to the woman with the red-brown eyes, whose springy, impatient movements were audible in the next room. Elizabeth hoped that Miss Berrington was not taking her mother's remarks to herself. It did not appear that the old lady had been thinking of her daughter when she spoke of Christians who brought troubles on themselves; nevertheless, Mrs. Berrington's little homily was certainly followed by an increase of rattling and stirring about in the kitchen.

However, nothing disagreeable was said when the tea-maker came in with her tray. As she was spreading a clean coarse white cloth over the table, there was a discreet tap at the door.

"Come in, Nelmont," said Miss Berrington, in no welcoming tones.

Nelmont entered, greeted the three ladies politely, and explained that he had set out to look for Miss Green.

"And a weary long time you have been engaged in the quest!" Miss Berrington said snappishly. "If Miss Green had been injured, she might well have been dead before you bestirred yourself to search for her."

Nel took the reproof coolly. His dark blue eyes glinted with mischief as he said: "Don't be cross, Berry. I couldn't come sooner, for the good reason that we did not miss Miss Green till a short time ago. And after that I had first to take Donnet home."

Miss Berrington uttered a contemptuous snort. "Why not say, straight out, that you dared not bring Donata here, neither dared Donata come?" she said. "Well, sit down and take your tea."

Chapter 9

BLACKBERRY TEA

WHATEVER Nelmont Deveril's other faults, it was not to be denied that he possessed a sweet temper. This was the opinion formed by Elizabeth during the meal that followed. Miss Berrington ate little herself, but spent the time in scolding Nel heartily, first for his cavalier treatment of Elizabeth and secondly for the bad behaviour that had earned him temporary banishment from Eton. To all these animadversions Nel returned no other answer than a teasing smile until, taking advantage of Miss Berrington's involuntary pause for breath, he observed mildly: "This catalogue of my sins isn't very entertaining for Miss Green, is it? I propose that we change the subject."

Miss Berrington glowered at him.

"I haven't mentioned what I strongly suspect to be the latest of your wrong-doings," she said. "I don't know whether you prompted my former pupil or whether she prompted you. But I assure you that I hold you both in very low esteem."

"Umm-m! Going to tell tales on us?" inquired Nel.

"Fortunately for the pair of you, it is no business of mine," said Miss Berrington, on a bitter note. "As far as I am concerned, you may do as you please."

"You are referring to *that*?" said Nel.

"Yes, I am referring to *that*," Miss Berrington answered tartly. "If you and Donata have other crimes on your consciences, I have not heard of them."

Elizabeth could not make out their meaning, but she noticed that they had each looked in turn significantly at Great-Aunt Georgina's stately riding-hat and gloves, which were lying on the sofa. She feared that in accepting the cousins' offer to teach her to ride she had done something that was considered to be not in keeping with the position she held at the Court. True, Mr. Cosmo had seen nothing amiss; but then Mr. Cosmo was only a man, and a young man at that, immersed in the cares of his estate and surrounded by a whirl of election business. An experienced governess like Miss Berrington was better qualified to pronounce on fine points of etiquette.

"Miss Berrington," she asked impulsively, "ought I not to ride? Is it wrong or inadvisable?"

"I see no objection," Miss Berrington answered coldly. "I accompany pupils myself, when it is required of me by an employer."

Elizabeth was forced to conclude that she had

been mistaken in supposing that she was in any way concerned in the glances that had lighted on Great-Aunt Georgina's property. Nel's misdeeds were numerous and notorious: probably he and Miss Berrington were speaking of some ill-doing now more than three weeks past.

Having spoken her mind as far as she intended to speak it, Miss Berrington became gracious, and showed herself for what she was, a clever and cultured woman, able to command liking as well as respect. It was with regret that Elizabeth had to take leave of mother and daughter, in order to be present at a lesson postponed to the evening by Donata's music master, a timid old gentleman whose pupil was wont to treat him with disrespect.

Nel was silent until they were riding down a lane at some distance from the cottage. Then he said abruptly:

"I've known Miss Berrington all my life. You have heard that she taught my brothers and me our first lessons? She's made like that, vinegar and spices. It's the result of her troubles. She has had to be the family prop, supporting invalid, aged, and ne'er-do-well relations in every conceivable calamity. As you have seen, she hasn't a great deal of money to do it on."

The interior of the cottage had told Elizabeth as much. Great-Aunt Georgina's feathers nodded in acquiescence.

"We do what we can. Always have," said Nel. "But she's as proud as an empress, and it is difficult to persuade her to accept any help. That accounts for——"

"It was a very good meal, I'm sure!" cried Elizabeth. "You must be hard to please if you are not satisfied with that sweet nutty home-baked bread and honeycomb from the garden bees."

"For myself, I would ask nothing better," said Nel. "But I dare say Mrs. Berrington would like a cup of tea, now and then, that wasn't made of blackberry leaves——"

"*Blackberry leaves?*"

"Yes, blackberry leaves. Don't pretend you haven't been puzzling your head to guess what the queer taste might be. I saw you trying not to wrinkle your mouth after the first sip! Blackberry leaf tea is all they can afford when Miss Dorothea Berrington is out of a job, as she is at present."

"Oh, I do feel such a supplanter!" mourned Elizabeth. "Miss Berrington is so much older and so—so everything that I am not. Learned, I mean, and witty and brilliant, and with such an air of authority. She ought to be at the Court instead of me. I am afraid she thinks so too."

"Not a doubt of it, she does. False modesty was never one of her failings."

"Ought I?—ought I to resign?"

"In her favour? Certainly not. You must have been told that she inconvenienced my mother very much by resigning without notice after a tremendous flare-up with Donnet. We all did our best to persuade her to reconsider her decision, but she flatly and utterly refused. That's the worst of a ginger-headed governess; it doesn't make for peace in the schoolroom."

"Mr. Nelmont!"

"Ten thousand apologies! I forgot you were one of the fraternity—or should it be sorority? Whichever it is, pray disabuse yourself of the notion that you have stepped unfairly into somebody else's shoes. They are yours by right, as Miss Berrington would be the first to acknowledge. She's a generous soul, really; she doesn't bear you any grudge."

"No, I am sure she doesn't," said Elizabeth. "I liked her and I liked her mother. They were both most kind to me. Did—did Donata dislike Miss Berrington excessively, do you know? She seems reluctant to speak of her."

"Ashamed of herself, that's why," quoth Nel. "No, I fancy it wasn't so much dislike as Donnet's rooted determination always to be 'top sawyer'. And that, where Miss Berrington's at hand, is impossible. Greek met Greek—and the tug-of-war burst the rope! My mother had to find a new rope. You are it."

Elizabeth rode on, without calling Mr. Nelmont's attention to the hybrid nature of his metaphors. She did not feel like a new rope. Her visit to the cottage had left her feeling like a length of cheap string.

"I don't know why you are so quiet, Miss Green," said Donata crossly, when the music lesson was over. "Were you hurt by your fall? What is the matter with you?"

"I was not hurt, and nothing is the matter," Elizabeth answered. "Except that I am unhappy about Miss Berrington."

"I'm sorry for her too," said Donata affably. "A volcanic temper is always a great trial to its possessor, is not it? And I cannot think how she can bear to live in a house haunted by the ghosts of at least a thousand pheasants that the boys have shot for her. Did you see the frightful screen and fans that she has made out of their feathers? Such touching evidence of her old pupils' devotion! But you didn't find any little offering from me, did you?"

Elizabeth would not answer the question. Scowling, Donata said: "There's no need for you to be unhappy. She may be poor, but she has enough to keep her and her mother from starving. And she was to blame for our falling-out, every bit as much as I was . . ."

Donata went on talking rapidly long after Elizabeth had ceased to listen. She was recalled from her thoughts by hearing Donata say loudly:

"Didn't Nel tell you that Miss Berrington wouldn't give way when they all begged her to change her mind?"

"Yes, he told me that."

"Well, then, why are you worrying yourself to skin and bones out of unnecessary tender-heartedness? She has gone for good, and you have come. And——"

"And what?" asked Elizabeth, when the pause showed no signs of ending.

"I never thought that I should ever live to say such a thing to a governess!" said Donata, ruefully. "It's as much a surprise to me as it will be to you. And after only three weeks, too! But I am going to say it. You've come—and I hope you'll stay!"

Chapter 10

LAVENDER MUSLIN

SIX weeks after her arrival at the Court, Elizabeth received an invitation to take tea at Watermill Farm.

It was such a hot Wednesday that the prospect of wearing Great-Aunt Georgina's frills and furbelows was unalluring. Elizabeth could not think that there was any need for her to look elderly and sedate in the house of Mrs. Watson, however desirable these qualities might be at Deveril Court. She took from her wardrobe the pretty never-worn lavender muslin that had been one of the two "leaving dresses" sent after her from Crowgarth's. Feeling young again she went gaily through the lanes.

The six weeks had been happy. Whatever the cause, Donata's manners had steadily improved since the first Sunday night when for a brief space Elizabeth had feared she would never be happy again. All the visiting masters had congratulated Miss Green on the marked improvement shown by her pupil; and Elizabeth's own lessons had met with a fair measure of attention and diligence, though from time to time Donata showed herself unaccountably sleepy in the mornings as well as not a little cross. Out of school she had been friendly, and had apparently modified her passion for rat-hunting, cross-country riding, and inciting Nel to defy guardians and elder brothers. Nel for his part had been much more amenable than Elizabeth had been led to suppose, neither haunting the schoolroom nor enticing Donata into madcap escapades, but spending his leisure hours in the by-election campaign, into which Cosmo and Ughtred had plunged with the utmost zest and which, being now at its height, occupied the major part of their days.

So Elizabeth had reason to look sunshiny as she tripped to the farm. Under the rose porch stood a little figure, joyously waving its arms. It came flying down the path to meet her.

"Tibbie! Tibbie! You're here, you're here!"

"I've come to live at Watermill Farm for always," proclaimed Tibbie. "I thought I was going away from Crowgarth's to be a governess like you. But I am nobody's governess. I am Grandfather's and Grandmother's little girl."

"That she is, bless her!" cried Mrs. Watson fondly. And when the hugs and kisses were over and Tibbie had dashed off to catch a kitten, Mrs. Watson turned to the guest.

"Oh, Miss Green, it was your psalm that *did it*, I shall always say. Mr. Watson's so obstinate, he will have it that 'twas the black crows in the lower pasture—the sight of them got on his brain, he said, and he couldn't rest for thinking of them——"

"But why should the black crows make Mr. Watson bring Tibbie home?" Elizabeth asked wonderingly.

Mrs. Watson coughed. "You'll excuse Mr. Watson, I'm sure. It was the name of the Orphanage, combined with the great black cloak you wore. The crows in the pasture did look so very like——"

"Oh, but you mustn't blame Mr. Charles Crowgarth for our black cloaks!" said Elizabeth anxiously. "In his day, we wore scarlet by his express desire. The Trustees changed the colour just before I went to the Orphanage, I believe. They said black was more fashionable."

"Well, it didn't suit Mr. Watson," said Mrs. Watson, "and, as I was remarking, every time he saw a crow it went and upset him by putting him in mind of Mary's little lass. But the crows were only an instrument, so to speak. Right at the back of them there was me praying for a patient mind. And oh, Miss Green, it isn't a patient mind any longer!—it's a rejoicing one."

Elizabeth rejoiced too. For one afternoon she threw off staidness and romped like a child with Tibbie in hayfield and meadow. And when Tibbie brought a brand-new skipping-rope to be admired, Elizabeth could not resist the temptation to use it. At Deveril Court the governess must sit soberly by when Nel and Donata played fives or battledore and shuttlecock. As for skipping, it was unthinkable. No governess ever skipped. But here among the haycocks she could be fifteen again if she pleased.

So she seized the rope and skipped pepper, salt, and mustard for the entertainment of Mrs. Watson and Tibbie, till the fun was brought to an end by the apparition of two gentlemen on horseback, riding along the highroad.

Down went the skipping-rope in a trice. Elizabeth clapped her hands to her flaming cheeks.

"Oh, oh! Mr. Cosmo and Mr. Ughtred Deveril!—they must have seen me! Oh, what will they think?"

"They have no call to think anything," said Mrs. Watson; "they know you are but a young thing after all."

"I hope they won't write to tell Mrs. Deveril that I am too young," said Elizabeth dolefully. "I am more afraid of Mr. Ughtred than of Mr. Cosmo. Though he is younger, he is more stern and disapproving."

Mrs. Watson did not say that Elizabeth was not nearly old enough for the responsible post she occupied in a household at present composed of two young men, a reckless youth, and a wild girl. Mrs. Deveril knew her own business best, opined Mrs. Watson; but with all due respect to Madam Deveril, it was a queer state of affairs she'd left behind her when she went to nurse her sick sister.

"But perhaps they didn't recognize me in my new dress," said Elizabeth hopefully. "It is not in the least like the clothes I wear at the Court, is it, Mrs. Watson?"

Mrs. Watson agreed that it was not; but Elizabeth's peace was not restored until she had met the Deveril brothers soon after her return to the Court, when she was once more resplendent in her borrowed plumes. Neither of them, she was glad to observe, wore the faintly amused air of a man who had recently seen a sober respectable governess skipping like a March hare in a hayfield. Mr. Cosmo was as pleasantly courteous as usual, Mr. Ughtred as haughtily indifferent.

In the evening Kitty came for her bi-weekly lesson, which progressed so well that teacher and pupil were alike delighted.

"I never thought I'd learn so quick!" said the gratified Kitty. "Why, if this goes on, I shall soon be as fond of reading as you and Miss Donata."

"Miss Donata!" Elizabeth echoed, in some mystification; for Donata seldom disturbed the contents of the schoolroom or library shelves.

"Why, yes, Miss! Often and often in the morning I've found books strewn on Miss Donata's bed, as if she'd been reading till she fell asleep."

The reason for Donata's morning drowsiness began to emerge. A further puzzle was solved late in the evening, when Elizabeth noticed a key sticking in the locked drawer of her bureau, where key had never been seen before. On turning it, she found that the drawer was full of novels.

The elder Crowgarthians had been allowed to read novels, carefully selected by Miss Tadcaster. Reared on *Waverley* and its successors, Elizabeth was sure that Miss Tadcaster would not approve of *Midnight Horrors*, *Phantom Hands*, *Conrad the Necromancer*, *The Fatal Bridal*, *The Spectre of Castle Angelo* and their companions. It was, she feared, significant that these volumes had not been claimed by their former owner, who had doubtless forgotten to take them away with her.

There was nothing to be done save to re-lock the drawer and hide the key among her own possessions. All the happiness of the afternoon had fled away. Elizabeth could not but feel depressed when she reflected on the ease with which Donata had avoided detection when she was doing what she must have known to be wrong. After preparing a remonstrance to be spoken as soon as Donata returned from the Wednesday visit to Grove House, Elizabeth sadly busied herself with the studies that were intended to keep her in advance of her pupil.

Work did not go well that evening. Her

thoughts were astray and refused to twine themselves round history and geography; her head ached with the struggle to learn enough for two people. She was thankful for the sudden remembrance that she had given Donata leave to go riding on the morrow in the unexceptionable company of Admiral Pretty's daughters, with whom Miss Deveril had struck up a violent friendship some weeks ago.

Though she inwardly marvelled at Donata's choice of friends, Elizabeth had been only too glad to encourage an intimacy with those patterns of young ladyhood. Moreover, the extra free time was of the greatest value for her own studies. It was a relief to be able to lay down the pen and the text-books in the pleasant consciousness that there was a breathing-space ahead on the morrow. She would practise instead, secure in the certainty that her peace would not be marred by Donata's critical comments on her chord-splitting and erratic time-keeping.

Tinkle-tinkle-tinkle sang the schoolroom pianoforte, tinkle-tinkle-tinkle patiently, hour after hour. It became at last evident that the carefully prepared remonstrance could not be delivered till the next day; for Donata did not trouble to say good night to her governess on her return from Grove House, but went to her own room and banged the door.

Chapter 11

NOT MUCH USE AS A GOVERNESS

AT the breakfast-table the next day Donata was silent and moody, and snarled at Nel in a way that caused Mr. Ughtred Deveril to assume his most supercilious expression. In the school-room, she spoke before Elizabeth could open her lips.

"Miss Green, I hate you. Weren't Mrs. Watson and Tibbie and Kitty and I enough for you? Why did you have to go preaching to Nel?"

In stammering astonishment, Elizabeth said: "I haven't—I never have."

"Yes, you must have. Because there has been a change in him, ever since you came. Every-body has noticed it. I tried not to notice at first—but now it's no good pretending any longer. No, he hasn't listened to anything his mother said or his godmother said or Cosmo said or his guardians said. He owned as much when I asked him. So that only leaves you. You've preached to him—and you've utterly and completely spoilt him!"

Elizabeth thought of the text, hymn, and

prayer that she had chosen for the cousins. She said, with some reluctance:

"Did you—did you show Mr. Nelmont something I wrote?" Donata turned dark red and looked almost as embarrassed as Elizabeth.

"Well, yes, I did once, a long time ago," she owned after a pause, unwillingly. "But that had nothing to do with the change. Nel said it hadn't."

"Then I do not know what you can mean," said Elizabeth. "I have hardly ever spoken to Mr. Nelmont Deveril except in your presence, unless it might be 'Good morning' or something of that kind. I did not talk with him on serious matters when we rode home together the day I was thrown. If you ask him, he will tell you so."

"I don't believe you. *Somebody* must have said something that made Nel pull up and turn over a new leaf and all the rest of it."

"God speaks directly to our hearts when He chooses," said Elizabeth. "He does not always speak through people."

"Oh, do stop dragging religion into everything! I tell you, Nel has been different with a difference that is somehow your fault, and he is going on getting differenter and differenter so that he will soon be simply unbearable. He actually intends writing to his guardians to apologize for his conduct and to beg to be sent back to Eton. And he disapproves of everything I do, now."

Elizabeth began to understand. "You mean, Mr. Nelmont knows that you had contrived to possess yourself of a key that fits the locked drawer? He thinks you ought not to be secretly helping yourself to the books in it?"

"Of course he does!" cried Donata, furiously. "Prig, miserable prig that he is! But fussing about those books isn't his only crime, nor his worst. Just when I was having such a happy, happy summer, he must needs begin behaving like Cosmo and Ughtred rolled into one."

Elizabeth was troubled. "If Mr. Nelmont disapproves of your behaviour, then you may be very sure that Mrs. Deveril would also disapprove. What have you been doing?"

"Wouldn't you like to know? Well, then, nothing that any person with a spark of liveliness or a spice of fun in him or her could possibly object to my doing! You need not look as though I had robbed a bank or set a house on fire. I've no reason to be ashamed of what I have done."

"If you are not ashamed of it, you will let me hear what it is. Indeed, you must explain. I am your governess, remember."

"Yes. So you are, Elizabeth Green, green Elizabeth. And a mighty verdant governess you are, Elizabeth Green, Fifteen! I don't intend to explain, so that's flat. All I will tell you is this: that Nel has finally and definitely refused to help me in hoodwinking you and

Cosmo. He has been very disagreeable about helping me for the last six weeks—and now he says 'Never again!' I could as easily overthrow a mountain as that hateful Nel. Don't care. I shall manage without him."

"I don't know what you can mean, Miss Deveril; but I shall think it my duty to watch you closely in future."

"By all means, Miss Green. Nature designed you for a mouser."

"Oh, please!" said Elizabeth, "don't let us quarrel. You would do the same, in my place."

"No, I wouldn't. I'd have a little pity on a girl who was trying to show everybody that she doesn't care in the least what the world thinks of her. For that's what it is, Miss Green. They all know now—Nel's friends, Cosmo, Ughtred, and Nel himself. Even blind Mrs. Vallard has heard it, and is being horrid to me. Those detestable Thompsons have spread the story about Rhoda and Willoughby everywhere, as I said they would."

"Oh, I am sorry!" said Elizabeth, "so very sorry."

Sympathy softened Donata; but she refused to listen when Elizabeth again pleaded with her to put wrong right, as far as she could, by writing to entreat Rhoda's forgiveness.

"Not I! Nel may choose to look a fool by climbing down and humbling himself and saying he's sorry—but you won't catch me following his example. I'm not going to slink about crestfallen—I shall carry it off with a high hand, you'll see! But you are a nice little creature after all, Miss Green, and I wish I hadn't been nasty to you just now. If you weren't my governess, I should really and truly enjoy having you for a friend."

"I am not much use as a governess, certainly," sighed Elizabeth. Involuntarily she glanced towards the bottom drawer of her bureau. Donata's eyes followed hers.

"How did you find out what was inside?" Donata asked, with a short laugh.

"You left your key in the lock."

"Glad I didn't do it sooner. I've read them all!"

Elizabeth said nothing.

"Go on, pitch into me, can't you?" said Donata. "Miss Berrington would have emitted blue fire and volumes of purple smoke. I must say you haven't her gifts. Poor old thing, her talents are being wasted just at present! Never mind, you'll improve with practice, no doubt."

"You happen to know that Miss Berrington is still out of a post?" asked Elizabeth.

There was some uneasiness in Donata's manner as she answered shortly: "Well, yes, I do know it. I've heard the boys discussing how they could help her without having their gifts flung back in their faces."

"Would Miss Berrington come back to the Court, do you suppose?"

"If the Deveril family went on its knees to her, yes!" said Donata. "The boys could wheedle her into returning to-morrow, if I didn't stand like a lion in the path. Ughtred would enjoy doing it, to pay me out for the trick I played on Rhoda. It would have to be the entire family in the dust, mark you. She wouldn't yield unless she saw me grovelling with the others. And that I never, never will. Never, do you hear? So you may as well get rid of any silly quixotic thoughts of making way for her. You've had them, I know you have, ever since the day you took tea in her cottage. But they are totally foolish, since I am quite as determined as she!"

Elizabeth was silent for a little while. Then she said:

"Am I to understand, once and for all, that you positively decline to explain in what ways you have 'hoodwinked' Mr. Cosmo Deveril and me?"

"Yes, my dear Miss Green, that is precisely what you are to understand, that and no less. And if you take my advice, you won't appeal to Cosmo. By doing so, you will completely spoil his enjoyment in having dead cats and rotten eggs thrown at him in his political meetings, and you will at the same time cause a general unpleasantness in the Deveril family.

Much better leave matters as they stand. Cousin Mildred will soon be at home to take charge of me herself. I may be able to outwit you and Cosmo, but I cannot hope to outwit her—and I shan't try. I shall reform, and be as meek as a sheep. So let well alone, my good governess, and don't meddle with what you can't mend."

Elizabeth did not answer.

"Are you going to hold the same threat over me that you held over me at the rat-hunt?"

"No," said Elizabeth slowly. "This time, I do not propose to appeal to Mr. Cosmo."

"I thought I could make you see sense," said Donata, well satisfied.

Nobody knew that for the rest of the day Elizabeth was fighting the severest temptation she had ever met.

She understood now, beyond possibility of mistake, that in accepting a position of authority over Donata she had undertaken a task above her powers. It was right that she should at once inform her employer of the melancholy discovery she had made.

But such a course would lead inevitably to her own dismissal. Would it be very wrong, Elizabeth asked herself, to keep silence about the past and the present, trusting in Donata's promise to be as meek as a sheep after Cousin Mildred's return? Mrs. Deveril was expected to return home shortly: there was really small likelihood of Donata's breaking out violently between this and then. Deprived of Nel's support, she would find it less easy to fulfil her boasts. Besides, even experienced governesses had—witness Miss Berrington!—occasional difficulty in controlling their pupils: there was surely no need to acquaint Mrs. Deveril with the history of a young beginner's first six weeks? What harm could there be in continuing to hold her post as long as she might?

Too restless to work during Donata's absence, Elizabeth went out for a solitary stroll as soon as she had seen Donata, with groom in attendance, soberly setting forth to her ride with the Misses Pretty. By way of motive, she carried in her hand the packet of paper dolls that she had brought with her to the Court. Tibbie had found in an oak tree an enchanting hole that would make, when duly carpeted with moss, a desirable residence for the little ladies. A promise had been given that they should be introduced to their new abode when next Elizabeth walked or rode past Watermill Farm.

Tibbie was not at home, although she could be seen, a dancing sprite, at play in the water meadows by her grandfather's side. Laying the dolls down on the moss, Elizabeth had a presentiment that for the second time she was presenting Tibbie with a farewell gift. She tried to shake off the unwelcome thought. The dolls should not be a farewell gift, no, they shouldn't! At the tea-party in the Berringtons' cottage, she had been told that old Mrs. Berrington knew how to fashion miniature sets of tables and chairs out of feathers. Why should she not visit Mrs. Berrington, and ask to be instructed in this domestic art? When her fingers were busy equipping the oak-tree house, she would forget foolish uncomfortable fancies.

Elizabeth did not admit, even to herself, that what she wanted at Violet Cottage was not the pattern of feather furniture, but counsel in her perplexity from one whose long life had shown her that the troubles even of Christian people were caused "by their relying on their own strength, putting their trust in themselves, and choosing their own way". Slowly and heavily she took the road for the common. At the last bend, sounds of music reached her ears.

Chapter 12

CAREFUL CONSIDERATION

ELIZABETH had hoped that Miss Berrington would be gathering fir cones or attending to the wants of the black hen. It was disappointing to find that she was at home, playing the piano. Still, it was possible that Mrs. Berrington might be in the garden, where a private talk could take place.

The distant sounds became sweeter, louder, and clearer as Elizabeth walked on. All in a moment, her steps faltered and stayed, her eyes shone, and she stood breathless. "Oh!" she said, half aloud, "oh, I did not know the instrument *could* sound like that!"

Elizabeth never knew how long she remained in the dusty little lane at the back of Miss Berrington's cottage. When the music stopped, she unclasped her hands and brushed tears from her eyes as if she were waking from enchanted dreams.

"Donata told me that Miss Berrington played much, much better than I did—but she never said that Miss Berrington played as if she would draw the moon out of the sky! I shall never be as good as she, if I practise for a thousand years."

There were two ways of approaching the cottage. With the mien of a pricked bubble, Elizabeth walked round to the front garden. Three horses were tethered to the fence where once she had tethered Snowball. She knew that Cosmo, Ughtred, and Nelmont must be calling on their old governess. They had found her at the pianoforte, and had been listening . . . Now they were telling her the latest news of the by-election that had absorbed so much of their time and thoughts lately. Miss Berrington's keen, clever face would be alight with interest as she discussed the prospects of the candidate and the future of his party.

"I can't play, and I don't know how to talk politics. Even Donata knows more about them than I do," thought Elizabeth. "I have set myself up for a governess when I am nearly as ignorant as Tibbie!"

She did not wait to see whether Mrs. Berrington was in the front garden, but turned and ran away, with Great-Aunt Georgina's third-best black silk trailing after her. Whatever counsel she took, must be taken now in the depths of her own soul.

Let this mind be in you, which is also in Christ Jesus. The words of her "leaving text" rang in Elizabeth's head as she pondered her problem. With it, like a refrain, rang some of the phrases from the collect that she had copied into the thought book for her own use: "serve Him with a quiet mind . . . a quiet mind . . . a quiet mind . . ."

"I am not sure," said Elizabeth, "that I could serve Him with a quiet mind if I went on hiding what I know from Mrs. Deveril for three more weeks, or two more weeks, or even one more week, whichever it may be."

At six o'clock Elizabeth was in the hottest part of the conflict. Her "I am not sure that . . ." had changed into "I am afraid I could not . . ."

In the late evening, the battle was won. "I am afraid I could not . . ." had become "I am convinced I could not . . ." The schoolroom lamp burnt long into the night while Elizabeth sat composing a letter:

"Dear Madam,

After careful consideration I deeply regret to tell you that I feel I am not filling my post satisfactorily.

In the first place, I have quite failed to exercise proper control over Miss Donata Deveril, though she has been good enough to say that she has no objection to me personally. I am sorrowfully obliged to confess that, unknown to me, she has been meeting throughout the time of my residence here, friends of whom you would not approve. I am unable to give you any further particulars; for she refuses to say where, how, or with whom, she contrives these meetings. Nor did I discover, till yesterday, that she had secretly obtained access to a drawer in my bureau filled with novels left behind by a former temporary governess. These, I am sorry to say, she has been reading in bed. Furthermore, I have been unable to induce her to apologize to her injured cousin, Miss Ponsonby.

In the second place, though I have striven diligently to remedy my defects, I fear that in certain subjects I cannot keep ahead of Miss Donata Deveril, whose intellect and accomplishments are much superior to mine. As she has frequently had occasion to observe, her French accent and pianoforte-playing surpass her governess's. I can see that her language and music masters agree with her.

The truth is, dear Madam, that I am both not clever enough and far too young. When I found that Miss Deveril disliked being taught by a girl of her own age, I readily accepted her suggestion that I should try to make myself look older by wearing the clothes bequeathed to her by her great-aunt; but even this practice has not given me the weight and authority without which the best teacher is helpless. In the circumstances, it would be unjust to blame Miss Deveril for misdemeanours that she could not have committed had she been in wiser keeping than mine.

As my best endeavours have been fruitless, I herewith resign my office, and I shall return to Crowgarth as soon as you can hear of a responsible lady to take my place. In this connection, I may remark that I could, if so desired, use what small modicum of influence I possess in persuading Miss

Donata Deveril to agree to the re-instatement of her former governess, the learned and talented Miss Berrington . . ."

Early the next morning the letter was dropped into the post-bag.

Elizabeth continued her teaching with a lump of lead in the spot that had once contained a heart. She did not tell her pupil what she had done. Two days went by.

Chapter 13

ALARMS AND EXCURSIONS

"DONATA," said Elizabeth, "you must really pay more attention to your studies. Pray refrain from constantly looking out of the window."

"There's a carriage coming up the drive," said Donata. "I want to see whose carriage it is. It looks rather like—oh-h-h! It *is* Uncle Charles's carriage! What can Uncle Charles be doing here?"

Pale with alarm, Donata sprang to the window to watch the opening of the coach door.

"Uncle Charles, Aunt Hester—and *Rhoda*!" she said in a faint voice. "I know why they have come. This is more of the Thompsons' work. They have written to Rhoda about my goings-on. She has told her parents, and they have come to find out why I am not being properly looked after in Cousin Mildred's house. So now all the skeletons will skip from their cupboards—oh, misery me!"

"What skeletons?" cried Elizabeth, in distress.

"Never you mind," said Donata. "You'll hear soon enough."

They both sat mutely listening. In a few minutes footsteps were heard approaching. The room was suddenly full of people. Mr. Cosmo Deveril, grave and perplexed, was speaking Elizabeth's name. She was dimly aware that she was being introduced to three grandly-dressed personages who were gazing at her with glacial severity. Behind them stood Ughtred and Nelmont Deveril, the one wearing his loftiest expression, the other looking very hangdog.

"You will excuse us, Miss Green," said Donata's Uncle Charles Ponsonby. "Some extremely odd rumours have reached my wife and me concerning the conduct of our niece, Miss Donata Deveril. I wish to put some questions to the young lady. Donata!"

Donata stood up. "Yes, Uncle Charles?"

"Is it true, Donata, that in company with your cousin, Mr. Nelmont Deveril, you have been visiting at houses in the neighbourhood without the knowledge or consent of your cousin Mrs. Deveril or of her son Mr. Cosmo Deveril?"

"As you know all about it already, I can't help admitting that it is true," said Donata gloomily. "But you are not to blame my governess, Miss Green. Except for a rat-hunt at Falfont Manor on the very next afternoon after her arrival, she knew nothing whatever about my excursions till the last time I went out, three days ago."

"It is a governess's duty to know that her

pupil is in the habit of escaping from the house at night," said Uncles Charles indignantly.

"Escaping from the house at night!" said Mr. Cosmo, with a kind of gasp.

"I only did it once, when I wanted to go to the Sutherlands' moonlight dance on their lawn," said Donata crossly. "I nearly fell off the roof of the porch after getting out of my window. And Nel said it should be the last time he would help me to do anything so dangerous—and it *was* the last time, so you needn't keep muttering 'Gross negligence,' to yourself. It happened in Miss Green's first week here, when nobody in his senses could have expected a new governess to be up to all my tricks."

From her place by the table, Elizabeth saw the assembled figures grouped as in a picture; they no longer seemed real. Mr. Cosmo and Mr. Ughtred Deveril were looking darkly on their brother and cousin. The elder Ponsonbys appeared to be swelling with wrath. Miss Rhoda Ponsonby wore an air of quiet satisfaction.

"And you can't blame Miss Green for anything that I did when I was supposed to be riding with the Pretty girls," Donata added, in the same defiant manner. "She used to see me off, with James in attendance. It was understood that he should take me as far as the Admiral's gates, and that the Prettys and their groom should accompany me to the Court gates on the return from the ride. How was she to know that I used to trot a little way up Admiral Pretty's drive and then turn down a side path that took me straight into the Greltham Road? Ride with the Prettys! —not me! I'd as soon ride with a string of suet puddings! And everything else happened on the afternoons and evenings of Sundays and Wednesdays, when Miss Green was not responsible for me. They were her free hours. Cousin Mildred and Cosmo arranged it, didn't you, Cosmo?"

Cosmo Deveril bowed his assent.

"I repeat, Sir, that I am in fault," said Nel, coming forward to address Mr. Ponsonby. "As I have already admitted, I frequently took Donata with me to the houses of my friends."

"What sort of orgies do you think I have been attending, pray?" said Donata, with a stamp of her foot. "The worst I have done is to dance and play cards, both of which I learnt to do in your house, Uncle Charles, before I ever set eyes on Nel or the Court. And Nel was very careful where he took me. If you want to hear how we did it, this is how. You see, I hide nothing, because I will not allow anybody to blame Miss Green. It was all quite simple. Sometimes Nel came to tea with his blind godmother, and then he would say that he was going to Falfont St. Philip to visit his grandparents, and could I come too? Of course, Mrs. Vallard saw no objection. And when we got to Falfont St. Philip, I would wait in his grandparents' garden until he had paid his respects to them. After chatting with them for half an hour, he would join me again and we would ride off together. At other times I would slip out of the arbour where Mrs. Vallard used to leave me alone for hours and hours reading dull old books. So it is as plain as a pikestaff that you cannot blame Miss Green."

Uncle Charles shifted the point of attack.

"I have been informed, Donata, that you have been reading, and lending among your friends, a number of novels unsuitable for perusal by young ladies."

"They were just what Rhoda reads, no better and no worse!" retorted Donata. "I found a key that fitted a locked drawer in the schoolroom. The books inside it had been there for years before Miss Green came, and she had no reason to suppose that I had got at them—why should she, when she hadn't the smallest suspicion that they were there at all? Obviously, you can't blame her for that, either."

"I hope I am too just to blame Miss Green for faults which are not hers," said Uncle Charles Ponsonby. "But I cannot help feeling that you would not have behaved so badly, had your governess set you a better example. I have been given to understand that Miss Green gallops all over the county with you and Mr. Nelmont Deveril. More shocking still, Miss Green is said to be a constant and successful competitor at the race-meetings privately organized by the young people of this neighbourhood, as well as a patron of a vulgar shooting-gallery in Falfont St. Philip and—I blush to say it—an expert thrower at coco-nuts at local fairs. Is this, may I ask, creditable conduct in a governess?"

"Oh, Uncle Charles, that was me!" interrupted Donata. "Miss Green has never galloped about the countryside, never. Purely to oblige me—and much against her own inclinations!—she has been learning to ride with Cosmo's full knowledge and approval. He will tell you, if you ask him, that poor Snowball still thinks she has got a sack of coals on her back! As for the races and the shooting-gallery and the fairs, I dared not attend them in my own person, for fear Cosmo or Ughtred or somebody should find out what I was doing and stop me. So I wore some of Miss Green's clothes, which were well known everywhere; for they amused people so much by their quaint old-fashioned cut. At least, they were not really Miss Green's clothes——"

Uncles Charles lifted a hand to ask for silence.

"That brings me to a question I particularly wish to ask Miss Green," he said, turning for the first time to Elizabeth. "Have the goodness, Madam, to account for the disguise in which I find you!"

"*Disguise!*" echoed Mr. Cosmo and Mr. Ughtred Deveril, blankly. Mr. Cosmo, colouring crimson, began to stammer incoherencies, from which Elizabeth gathered that he was trying to remind the Ponsonbys, as tactfully as he could on the spur of the moment, that governesses were not always so fortunate as to be able to choose the contents of their wardrobes. When ill paid, they were sometimes reduced to accepting the cast-off finery of their friends. She was grateful to him for having taken this charitable view of her amazing taste in dress; but before he had stumbled to the end of his explanation, Nel broke in.

"I am to blame again, Sir!" he said to Mr. Ponsonby. "As you have perhaps realized, Miss Green is rather young to be the governess of a girl as old as Donata. When she arrived at the Court, Donata was for refusing to be taught by Miss Green. I am ashamed to say that I pointed out privately to Donata the advantages of having only a very inexperienced young lady in charge of her. So——"

"The rest of it is as much my fault as Nel's!" shouted Donata. "All he did, was just to convince me that Cosmo would insist on Miss Green's being sent away and replaced by an older and more sedate person—that he would declare it wasn't suitable to have a couple of giddy girls chaperoning each other in a houseful of young men. And when I began to want her to stop, I didn't see how it was to be managed unless I could contrive to make her look older than she was. So I lent her some of Great-Aunt

Georgina's clothes. I was quite sure that Cosmo would be taken in—as he was! When he saw how hideously she was dressed, he hardly ever looked her way again, for fear of seeming to stare at her. As for Ughtred, he took no more notice of her than of a fly on the ceiling—nobody would ever expect him to look twice at the old-fashioned frump who had sat herself down in dear Miss Berrington's place! But indeed and indeed, Miss Green herself had not the least notion that she was deceiving anyone. She humoured me because her Miss Tadpole had said she ought always to dress as soberly as a woman of sixty-five, or words to that effect. She comes from an Orphanage, and she has as much knowledge of the world as a pink-tipped white daisy. And she never dreamt that Cousin Mildred would never have engaged her if she had known she was only fifteen——"

"FIFTEEN!" cried Cosmo, as if thunder-struck. "Miss Green, is it possible——?"

The momentary pause gave Elizabeth time to speak. She faced her judges bravely.

"I am very sorry that I have been so stupid. As soon as I arrived, I found that both Miss Tadcaster and I had been mistaken in the age of my pupil. In the agitation, doubtless, of receiving the anxious news about her sister, Mrs. Deveril omitted that important particular. Of course, it ought to have occurred to me that Mrs. Deveril would naturally be expecting Miss

Tadcaster to send an older governess for a girl of fifteen; but Miss Donata Deveril speaks truly when she assures you that—that I didn't think of it. And—and I tried hard to give satisfaction, but my youth and inexperience have been against me."

"I am sure, Miss Green——" began Cosmo, and stopped with a look that showed that he was sure he did not know what to say next.

"Mr. Deveril need not put himself to the pain of dismissing me," said Elizabeth. "Three days ago, on becoming aware of the full extent of my dreadful failure, I wrote to Mrs. Deveril and resigned my post. In the letter I stated that I would remain in temporary charge of Miss Donata Deveril until Mrs. Deveril was able to replace me by Miss Berrington or some other person. May I suggest that Miss Berrington be—be consulted immediately? I—I understand that she only awaits Miss Deveril's submission——"

"Donata," said Cosmo sternly, "are you willing to apologize?"

"I—I suppose I must," Donata muttered. "Yes."

"Then there is no need for me to stay at the Court any longer," said Elizabeth, with quivering lips. "But before I go, I should like to mention some proofs that I did not purposely deceive my employers about my age. Mrs. Berrington, Miss Berrington, and Mrs. Watson of Watermill Farm can testify that I did not hide it from them. And if by any chance Mrs. Deveril has preserved my letter of resignation, it will prove, I think, that I did not know I was doing anything questionable. I—I hope that Mr. Deveril will later read what I wrote, Mr. and Mrs. Ponsonby also. And now, if you will all excuse me, I will withdraw to prepare for leaving by the afternoon coach."

Chapter 14

WITH A QUIET MIND

ALONE in her room, Elizabeth tearfully set about her packing. From the schoolroom came a confused angry sound of rebuke, remonstrance, debate. Now and then the rebukers and debaters became so impassioned that Elizabeth put her fingers into her ears and held her breath for fright. Gradually the storm died down. Footsteps were heard in retreat. The schoolroom fell silent.

Then Donata's scared face appeared in the doorway. She halted there, doubtful of her reception.

"Come in," said Elizabeth.

Downcast and wonderfully subdued, Donata came.

"They have gone—all save Nel—to interview Miss Berrington," Donata announced wretchedly.

"I am glad you were able to apologize."

"I can't think how you can be glad about anything! Oh dear, I did try so hard to save you, but I knew all the time it wasn't any good—they would never let me keep you. And, oh, what a mercy you had written that letter! When he heard of it, Ughtred's feelings were softened. Even Uncle Charles seemed pleased that you were not as black as you had been painted. And Cosmo became as stiff as a poker, and said he was bitterly ashamed of the way you had been treated in his house. He made as if he were speaking to Nel and me—but it was a hit at Uncle Charles as well. I think that was why Uncle Charles hit back by insisting on himself going to inspect Miss Berrington to see whether she was a fit governess for me! Cosmo and Ughtred are hoping to persuade her to shut Violet Cottage and bring her mother here to stay till Cousin Mildred's return, whenever that may be."

"And you will be good, Donata?"

"For your sake, I will, and for my own, too. You've worked on my conscience. I'm *glad* to be sorry: oh, but I don't want to lose you . . . Cosmo sent a message. He hopes you quite understood why he didn't ask you to stay till his mother came home. He couldn't ask, partly because the Ponsonbys wouldn't have allowed it, and partly because you are too young to stay here without an older lady at the head of affairs. Mrs. Hunt is no use—I heard him saying under his breath she was a nonentity. He's rather cross with her, too, for not having had the sense to warn him that you were not as old as you looked. She must have known, he says, and why didn't she speak! And he trusts you will consent to delay your departure till after he comes back from Violet Cottage, when Mrs. Hunt will escort you—oh, dear!—to Crowgarth's by post chaise. Will you, he says, be kind enough to receive him in the schoolroom before you leave? I think he wants to tell you how sorry he is that you have suffered hard things from Nel and me, and to assure you that you are quite perfectly cleared from any suspicion of having been in league with us to deceive him. You need not be afraid to meet Cosmo. I never liked him so much, or Ughtred either. They were both very understanding."

"Pray thank Mr. Cosmo for me," said Elizabeth, shakily. "I—I would rather not wait to see him. I prefer to be gone before he returns from the visit to Miss Berrington."

Donata burst into tears.

"Oh, what a miserable girl I am! It's all my wicked self-will! I do like you so much—and now you're leaving me, and I shall never see you again!"

"Do you like me? Really and indeed?" said Elizabeth, as well as she could for the lump in her throat.

"Yes, of course I do! I should like to have had you for an own, own sister. I wish we were twins. You would have made the dearest second self, and you would have turned me into a better first self."

They kissed each other and cried in company.

"I never meant this to happen!" sobbed

Donata. "I didn't, I didn't! I always thought that Cousin Mildred would come home long before there was an explosion of any kind, and Nel and I meant to coax her into keeping you even though you were too young. We could have arranged it, I know we could. And I told you, did not I, that I meant to be good when she came? This horrible disaster is partly her fault, for staying away such an interminable time to nurse her sister. No, it isn't. Nobody is to blame save me. I love you—and I've been cruel to you quite by mistake!"

"It is best that I should go," said Elizabeth. "As I told Mrs. Deveril in my letter and Mr. Cosmo just now in the schoolroom, I have failed in everything I tried to do."

"I don't know what you call failure," said Donata, still sobbing, "when you think what you have done for Nel. He is changed, utterly changed—and it is you who are responsible for the change. Why, to-day, instead of laughing and being rebellious, he owned that he had done wrong! And he has apologized to Uncle Charles and to Cosmo. Apologized!—*Nel!* He wouldn't have done it a few weeks ago. And he didn't fly into a rage when they and Ughtred told him what they thought of him. Oh, how angry they were! They said such things! If I had been Nel, I never could have endured to stand there without saying a word in self-defence. I stuck up for myself, as you heard. Nel didn't."

"I am happy to hear of the change in Mr. Nelmont," said Elizabeth; "but I am still unable to guess what you mean by saying I had a hand in it. I say again, that I never spoke to him on religious matters."

"You may not have *spoken*," said Donata, "but—but look at this." She pulled a folded sheet of paper from her pocket. "Nel gave it to me as I was leaving the schoolroom. He said that he should not need the original any longer, as he had made a copy for himself."

To her astonishment, Elizabeth beheld the text, hymn, and prayer she had written at Donata's request on the first Sunday evening at Deveril Court.

"Mr. Nelmont had this all the time?" she said, bewildered. "But I asked you whether you had shown him what I wrote. You answered that you had shown it, but that he himself averred it had nothing to do with the change."

Donata wriggled in discomfort. "When I said that, we were at cross purposes. I believed you to be referring to your 'thought book'. Oh me, how my sins do keep on getting found out! The truth is, I stole your thought book on the first Sunday evening while you were busy thinking about what I had asked you to write. I took the thought book down to Mrs. Hunt's room, and later I turned it into ridicule to amuse her and Nel. It didn't amuse Nel the least little scrap. He snatched it from me and bolted. We had a round-the-world chase and a hot quarrel. If I had been a boy, he would have punched my head—he said so. In the end, I had to promise never to be such an obnoxious little wretch again. He put the book back himself, choosing a time when you were not in the room. The sheet was lying on the table. He knew what it must be, and he took it away and kept it because I was in such a vile temper he couldn't trust me to keep my promise."

"Mr. Nelmont took it away? Not you?" said Elizabeth, slowly following Donata's rapid explanation. "Well, what then?"

"I was puzzled, afterwards, when I couldn't see any sign of the paper you had promised to write. I concluded that you must have changed your mind about writing it; but I couldn't pluck up courage to ask you. I was afraid that if I asked about the paper, you might proceed to ask me in return what reason I had for borrowing your thought book without leave. As far as I knew, you hadn't seen it go, but you might have missed it later in the evening. So I said nothing, which was what Nel hoped I would do. He read the paper, and it made him think. All these weeks his thoughts have been getting more and more uncomfortable—and at last there came a day when he made up his mind to take action. I don't know what he meant; for he didn't say."

But Elizabeth knew. A line in the hymn had

been heavily underscored with a pen-stroke that was certainly not hers:

"*Christ, be Lord, be King to me!*"

In making those simple words his own, Nelmont Deveril had stopped walking in the wrong direction: he had swung round and taken his first step in the "journey of a thousand miles".

"So that's what you did for Nel," said Donata. "And you need not say you have failed, now you know you have helped Nel who was everybody's despair."

A gleam shone in Elizabeth's darkness. But she only said wistfully: "I am comforted to hear it, but—I haven't done anything for you, Donnet. I wish I could have helped you too."

Donata's hand was slipped into Elizabeth's. "Nel had your paper for six weeks. I have had it for ten minutes. There's a chance yet. . . ."

They were quiet for a little while.

"You have helped me in other ways, Elizabeth," said Donata softly. "To-day, for example. When the Ponsonbys had gone stalking off with Cosmo and Ughtred, I suddenly thought how pleasant it would be to escape from the fuss and perturbation by coaxing Nel to smuggle me away to dear Cousin Mildred, out of reach of the claws of my furious relatives and Miss Berrington. But I didn't. I stopped at home to face the music as firmly as he faced it during those horrid minutes in the schoolroom. And very unpleasant music it is going to be. Uncle Charles, Aunt Hester, Rhoda, Cosmo, and Ughtred will give Miss Berrington strict orders to make my life a burden to me in all sorts of awful ways. How she will enjoy doing it! She never thought she would have the chance, that day when you and Nel had tea in Violet Cottage and you listened, so innocent and puzzled, to what she said to him about the wickedness of our disguising you in Great-Aunt Georgina's clothes! She will grind an apology out of me to Rhoda, that will be her first proceeding . . . No, it shan't be! As I am telling nearly everybody in the world that I am sorry, I won't leave Rhoda out. Elizabeth, I promise faithfully that I will speak to her to-day. There!—will that comfort you a little bit?"

Elizabeth tried to speak, but could not.

"Oh, I don't know that I can bear all the grim looks when you are gone and I am alone!" said Donata.

"Where is Mr. Nelmont now?" asked Elizabeth apprehensively.

Donata smiled a puckered smile. "You're afraid that my good resolutions will waver? No fear of that! The new Nel wouldn't gallop off with me to Cousin Mildred—no, not if I begged him on my bended knees! You needn't worry your head about that. I'll remain here to await the onslaught of the Berrington. Nel asked me to say good-bye for him. He isn't at home.

Directly the row was over and done with, he went off by himself for a very long ride."

Elizabeth was once more Fifteen, Elizabeth Green. For some days she wandered about Crowgarth's like a forlorn little ghost. In seven weeks, all had changed. Her friends had formed new friendships; her "babies" were hers no longer, and away at Watermill Farm Tibbie played happily with the second farewell gift. Though Miss Tadcaster had been kind, she had pointed out Elizabeth's mistakes, had rebuked her for a sad lack of common sense, and had shaken her head over her pupil's darkened future. With each passing hour, it became harder for Elizabeth to take to herself the advice she had once given to Mrs. Watson. It was not easy to rest in the Lord and commit one's way unto Him when she was perpetually threatened with the same fate that had befallen that other failure, Laura Knowles. She had heard whispers of two elderly ladies who had applied to Miss Tadcaster for a companion. One was named Mrs. Elphinstone, the other Mrs. Sprott. Elizabeth's spirit quailed within her at the mere mention of either of them.

On the fourth day Elizabeth was in the linen room, mending torn sheets. Up the corridor came Miss Tadcaster, calling for Elizabeth Green.

Once more Fifteen's fate was in the balance. In the moment before she answered the call, she had time to fortify herself with part of her "leaving hymn"

> "Plant, and root, and fix in me
> All the mind that was in Thee . . .
> When 'tis deeply rooted here,
> Perfect love shall cast out fear;
> Fear doth servile spirits bind;
> Jesu's is a noble mind."

She ran out, saying to herself: "I won't have a servile spirit, I won't, I won't. It has been servile long enough, four whole days. Whether it is Mrs. Sprott or Mrs. Elphinstone, 'I will trust, and not be afraid'."

"I have found what I believe to be an easier post for you, Elizabeth Green," said the Superintendent. "This time you will be going out, not as a governess but as a companion——"

Elizabeth curtsied submissively. Before her tear-misted eyes swam a visionary procession of old ladies, muffs, bath-chairs, poodles, sleek pussies, and skeins of wool.

"—to a girl of your own age, with whom you will share an excellent daily governess and visiting masters," went on Miss Tadcaster. "The young lady needs, I hear, the spur of emulation and the silken rein of well-principled female companionship. I trust, Elizabeth, that you will make the best use of an arrangement that affords you not only unparalleled opportunities of perfecting your education, but also much better prospects of happiness than you have reason to expect after your late regrettable failure, for which, however, I am now inclined to blame you less than I did at first. Your future employer awaits you in my study."

Elizabeth curtsied again and followed Miss Tadcaster. As she did so, she observed with surprise that the leaden substance in her bosom had turned into an object that distinctly resembled a heart.

"So this is Elizabeth Green?" said the tall, majestic, grey-clad lady with whom her future lay. "I am glad to see you. Do you know, you were earnestly recommended to me by someone who took a very long ride to tell me all about you?"

Elizabeth's heart gave such a mad leap that it nearly shot out of her body. She laced her fingers tightly over it to keep it still, and said to herself severely: "Nonsense, fantastic nonsense! You misunderstood what was said; you cannot have heard it correctly. Miss Tadcaster is not smiling, nor is the lady. Do not permit yourself to fancy what could never be true."

"Are you ready to come with me at once, Elizabeth? Your young friend-to-be is awaiting you at the inn. She longs to see you."

Elizabeth and her luggage were ready in no time. While she put on her bonnet, Elizabeth said to herself: "I cannot think why I did not ask and why Miss Tadcaster did not tell me, whether the lady is Mrs. Sprott or Mrs. Elphinstone . . . It is Mrs. Elphinstone, I am positive . . . No, after all I believe she is Mrs. Sprott."

But every time she said the names, her eyes grew brighter.

Now the porter was marshalling Elizabeth's box to the inn. From the entrance of Crowgarth's Miss Tadcaster was fluttering a handkerchief. They had turned the corner and were in the market square, within sight of the inn.

Outside the inn door a girl with clouds of golden hair stood talking to a boy and a young man on horseback. Beyond them was a large chaise, with a second young man in the driver's seat. At sight of Elizabeth they all waved a welcome.

Then the lady who was neither Mrs. Sprott nor Mrs. Elphinstone looked down at Elizabeth with a smile that gave all doubts an answer of peace. Elizabeth Green went forward with a quiet and constant mind.